Praise for

I'm Happy for You (Sort Of...)

"Kay Wills Wyma once again champions a much-needed ——— and with heartfelt insight she challenges us to choose contentment over comparison. *I'm Happy for You* gently exposes the growing obsession with self-promotion and one-upmanship that's wearing us all out and, thankfully, offers wise solutions."

—TRACEY EYSTER, author of *Be the Mom* and *Beautiful Mess*

"Kay Wills Wyma captured my attention with her belly-laughing good storytelling steeped in reality as she tackled a question that's long overdue for an honest answer: What should we do about this comparison trap we find ourselves falling into daily? When comparison steals contentment, it's a problem that demands a solution. Kay gives it to us in a way that is easy on the heart and good for the soul."

—ELISA PULLIAM, author and life coach

"Who knew comparison was so prevalent and destructive? Awakening to this alone is worth the time invested in reading this honest and sometimes raw literary gem. Comparison's thievery of joy is arrested by the 'just let it go' practicality Kay offers so transparently and humorously."

—ROBIN POU, executive coach and attorney mediator;
coauthor of *Performance Intelligence at Work*

"Kay Wyma has managed to address what we're all dealing with on a daily basis—the ability to instantly compare our life to someone else's with a mere look at our phone. There we can see all the ways we are failing to be the best mom, the best wife, the best friend . . . and the list goes on. In the pages of *I'm Happy for You,* Kay offers insight into why we do this and how we can stop the cycle. If you're looking to live a life of contentment and authenticity and to be okay when your kid is the C student and not the valedictorian, you'll find comfort and realistic solutions in this book."

—MELANIE SHANKLE, *New York Times* best-selling
author of *Sparkly Green Earrings*

"*I'm Happy for You* is honest and funny, while tackling a serious problem that is stealing our joy: comparison. Kay creatively uses stories and personal confession to reveal the pitfalls of comparing, while offering a solid

ladder—built on godly wisdom—to help us climb out of that pit. . . .
There's freedom on these pages."

—JENNIFER DUKES LEE, author of *Love Idol*

"Kay Wyma hit a home run on the Focus on the Family radio program
when she talked about ways moms can combat the entitlement mentality
in their kids. In her new book, she scores another hit with an insightful
discussion of the pitfalls of comparing your life to others, especially
through social media. Her advice is timely and relevant."

—JIM DALY, president of Focus on the Family

"Victims of comparison drive-bys litter the Internet. There are virtual
warehouses of new ways to covet your neighbor's home, decorating skills,
summer vacation plans, or Pinterest-perfect kids' birthday parties. In this
paralyzing culture of obsessive comparisons, this book is the detox we all
need. With a sense of humor and an unrelenting honesty, Kay walks us
through the steps to finding our worth again in the God who never com-
pares us but always only calls us by name."

—LISA-JO BAKER, community manager for (in)courage;
author of *Surprised by Motherhood*

"With both cultural relevance and biblical foundation, Kay Wills Wyma
accurately defines the comparison problem and offers a solution. *I'm
Happy for You* is a must-read for anyone caught in the comparison trap."

—JOSHUA BECKER, founder of Becoming Minimalist

"The pursuit of bigger, better, newer, and more never stops. With a com-
pelling lilt, Kay Wills Wyma's pen pulls us along only to expose and
confront our comparison battle. From one co-struggler to another, Kay
brings us perspective and relief."

—Dr. MICHAEL EASLEY, former president of Moody Bible
Institute; teaching pastor; host of Michael Easley inContext

"Kay Wills Wyma has opened a powerful window on the reality of comparison and how it's impacting all of us, including vulnerable young lives.
With social media, instead of just keeping up with the Joneses, we're now
keeping up with the world. Kay navigates us through the pressures we all
face and teaches us how to be genuinely happy for others."

—KATHY IRELAND, CEO at kathy ireland Worldwide

I'm Happy for You

for You

{SORT OF... Not Really}

FINDING CONTENTMENT
IN A CULTURE OF COMPARISON

Kay Wills Wyma

WATERBROOK
PRESS

I'm Happy for You (Sort Of . . . Not Really)
Published by WaterBrook Press
12265 Oracle Boulevard, Suite 200
Colorado Springs, Colorado 80921

Details in some anecdotes and stories have been changed to protect the identities of the persons involved.

Trade Paperback ISBN 978-1-60142-595-9
eBook ISBN 978-1-60142-596-6

Cover design by Mark D. Ford. Cover photos by K. Krebs | plainpicture; Superstock; and Glow Images

Published in the United States by WaterBrook Multnomah, an imprint of the Crown Publishing Group, a division of Penguin Random House LLC, New York.

WaterBrook and its deer colophon are registered trademarks of Penguin Random House LLC.

Library of Congress Cataloging-in-Publication Data
Wyma, Kay Wills.
    I'm happy for you (sort of . . . not really) : finding contentment in a culture of comparison /
Kay Wills Wyma. — First Edition.
        pages cm
    Includes bibliographical references.
    ISBN 978-1-60142-595-9 — ISBN 978-1-60142-596-6 (electronic) 1. Contentment—
Religious aspects—Christianity. 2. Christianity and culture. I. Title.
    BV4647.C7W96 2015
    261—dc23

                                        2014045933

Printed in the United States of America
2015—First Edition

10 9 8 7 6 5 4 3 2 1

Special Sales
Most WaterBrook Multnomah books are available at special quantity discounts when purchased in bulk by corporations, organizations, and special-interest groups. Custom imprinting or excerpting can also be done to fit special needs. For information, please e-mail SpecialMarkets @WaterBrookMultnomah.com or call 1-800-603-7051.

To anyone who has ever endured junior-high
insecurities, even as an adult.

To everyone else: Really?

Contents

Contents

Obsessive Comparison Disorder

A Sign of the Times

> It isn't what you have or who you are or
> where you are or what you are doing that
> makes you happy or unhappy. It is what you
> think about it.
>
> —Dale Carnegie

My day hits an unexpected lull. All is quiet on the home front. And what's a person to do amid peace and quiet? Clean the house? Address and send envelopes containing Christmas cards from this and the past two years—before July? Get stuff done?

No, of course not.

"Quiet" signals a prime opportunity to waste time on the Internet. So I check my e-mail. Then I click on Facebook to get caught up on what all my friends have been doing.

I see that Jennifer, who writes beautiful coffee-table books, is on tour to promote her latest release. I learn a thing or two from articles shared by Jeff—something on cute koalas and a "Top 25" list of critically important factors related to abundant living. And I enjoy stopping by a swanky local charity event while in my pajamas. Jon and I aren't swanky, so we normally don't attend such events. But seeing the photos leads me to wonder whether we could or should have gone. Were we supposed to? Did we miss out? *No.* But somehow I'm tempted to believe otherwise, and I struggle a bit to be happy for all those other people having fun.

Realizing I don't need to travel any farther down this road of comparison but not wanting to think too long about why it bothers me, I decide to click my way to another site. The teaser for an article catches my attention. The link takes me to my old friend the *Financial Times,* something I rarely read these days, as it belongs to my former career and my pre-kid life. But the idea of sinking into an intelligent business-oriented article feels like slipping on a comfy old shoe. Well, until my brain bumps up against words like *derivative* and *macroeconomic* blah-de-blah-blah. Then I just pretend to understand and reassure myself that I used to know what all that stuff meant.

But today as I click to read, I'm met with a roadblock: "Please log in."

Apparently I can't read the article unless I'm a subscriber.

No worries. There are several options for subscribing, one of which provides limited access (three articles per month) for free. The magazine simply needs answers to some questions and a few boxes checked. Looks easy enough.

I sail through the first few data fields: *E-mail Address, Password, Country,* and *Zip Code.* But I stall at the next: *Your Position.* Instead of a simple fill-in-the-blank field, a pop-up menu provides a plethora of options from which to choose. Without analyzing the choices to find a fit, I quickly search for *Other.* I'm comfortable with *Other.* I wear a lot of different hats these days, but the title that most often comes into play is *Mother (other* with an *M).* But *Other* isn't there.

Missing Answer blinks at me in red, preventing access as it politely insists, *Please select your position.* Apparently, in order to read an article, I have to be somebody.

This little exercise is beginning to sting.

I try to find a category I can claim without lying.

- **Analyst.** Maybe. But at this age, I'd prefer something with a little more prestige.
- **Associate.** Could work. Sure, my office has four wheels, seems to always be running on empty, and is filled with stray wrappers and cups from various fast-food eateries. But meetings convene daily. I could do Associate.
- **Manager/Supervisor.** Should we add referee, motivational speaker, counselor . . . ?
- **Other C Level (CFO/COO/CIO/CMO).** Not sure what CMO is, but the rest, yes.
- **Professional.** Sadly, no. As confirmed by a daily soundtrack of "Mahhwwmm! You're *so* embarrassing!"
- **Programme / Project Manager.** Definitely. "Get your shoes; you have basketball in five minutes!" "Isn't that book report due tomorrow?" "Where's your lunch?"

- **Senior Manager / Department Head.** Yes. "Until you're out of this house, I am in fact the boss of you." "Because I said so."

- **VP/Director.** Always. "I don't care if you sat in the back last time! You can sit there again." "Quit whining!"

I decide to select *CFO/COO/CIO/CMO*. I mean how can I go wrong with so many initials? And eventually, I access the article. But by then I no longer care. Such self-assessment exercises can do that to a person. Contentment darts out of reach in these moments, regardless of titles. Ever elusive "enough"—as compared to others and our own expectations, or simply measuring up—dangles just out of reach.

Apparently, I'm not alone. I recently watched one of my kids walk a similar road in which data fields demanded to define his life—or so it seemed. He had asked me to help him register for a college entrance exam. To better understand the situation, I logged into the kid's SAT account while he was at school. I stared at the password prompt, wondering what he might have used when he tried to do this himself. I typed in our Amazon password and was instantly transported to his account, thankful for our family's general lack of creativity.

I was floored. Page after page of required information stared back at me.

Beyond name, social security number, address, and photo for identification purposes, a potential test taker gets to recount his life history. Every class, every grade, every extracurricular activity, every interest, every aspiration. It took me an hour to peruse the pages. My stomach hurt as I saw years of hard work summed up by a checked box. A checked box in a sea of unchecked boxes. Because no one can check them all.

Not every opportunity to size ourselves up comes as boldly as boxes begging to be checked. Such occasions lurk everywhere—in the carpool line, at the grocery store, in front of a computer screen, at church, and in the office—inviting us to assess our surroundings and see how we measure up.

When I talked with my teen about the test form, I tried to shift his focus to the positive. "Don't think about what others are doing. You're fine. Those boxes don't define you." And yet I couldn't help but wonder: *Is it possible to have peace in the midst of relentless pressures to compare?*

Obsessive Comparison Disorder

The thing is, for much of my life, I wouldn't have considered myself tethered to comparison. Besides the normal middle school insecurities and issues with outward appearance in my teens, I never really cared what people thought about me. I assumed my comfortable-in-my-own-skin mentality made me relatively impervious to comparison. Other people compare, but not me. (No need to point out that my simple assessment is formed by comparison.) I would find myself feeling a bit sorry for them and happy I couldn't relate.

At times I suspected its unsettling permeation, but I had never gone so far as to actually call it out and name it. Until my eyes started to see and I began to become aware of all the ways comparison reaches its tentacles into our culture, into our homes, into our moment-by-moment thought patterns.

Think about it: When was the last time you walked into an event, whether social- or business-related, and didn't do a quick scan to size up the crowd? Maybe to see who's there and determine your own worthiness to attend. Maybe to compare attire and gauge the suitability of your own. Or maybe you did a quick survey to find someone familiar to stand with so you wouldn't look like a lonely loser. Because you know that others are scanning too, checking where they fall in the lineup. In short, they're comparing themselves to you.

We do it all the time. In fact, whether we believe it or not, there are very few times we *aren't* comparing. We even compare ourselves to ourselves—our expectations, our perceptions, our dreams. Paul Angone, the popular author of *101 Secrets for Your Twenties,* calls comparison "the smallpox of our [the Millennial] generation."

What's Obsessive Comparison Disorder, you ask? It's the new OCD I've coined to describe our compulsion to constantly compare ourselves with others, producing unwanted thoughts and feelings that drive us into depression, consumption, anxiety and all-around discontent. It encourages us to stay up late on Facebook [poring] through all 348 pictures of our frenemies' "My Life Is Better Than Yours" album, and then it sends us to bed wondering why we feel so anxious.

Obsessively comparing yourself to others, becoming more and more frustrated that your life doesn't look like theirs, is the absolute most effective way to take your crisis to unhealthy, eating raw cookie dough with a serving spoon, levels. Like having to run outside to light up a cigarette, our comparison addiction is uncontrollable, and it is killing us.[1]

Well said. I'd also add that comparison's impact is not restricted to a certain generation, and it's not all social-media driven.

One evening not long ago my husband, Jon, and I attended a gathering at the home of some friends here in Dallas. I spotted a couple who had recently moved back to the area from Nashville and made my way across the room to hug them. As we chatted, they told us about the home they had bought and were remodeling while they and their son lived in its garage apartment. Standing in our host's lovely living room, the husband shared some of his insecurity about their own housing choices.

"We love where we're living," he told me, "but we drive over here and see kids playing outside. Then I think about *our* neighbors, the youngest of which is, um, around ninety, and I start to worry about Jackson having friends to play with. Which I know is ridiculous since he's almost past that age. But then I look at this house, which is larger than ours. And our perfect-for-our-family-of-three home seems pretty small, which is silly because it's fine. More than fine. It's crazy how quickly thoughts can travel to discontent."

Honestly, I was surprised. Few people have it all together like this guy does.

Right about then, my eye landed on a lovely work of art hanging on one of our host's walls. And I remembered that only moments earlier I might have—okay, I definitely had—longingly gazed at a butterfly sculpture above the stove in her kitchen and wished it hung in my kitchen. And my thoughts moved to my walls, a few still sporting prints that date back to my days as a single apartment dweller with barely a penny to my name. A framed print of Monet's water lilies has traveled with me from Washington, DC, to Dallas and my every move in between.

I cringed at the thought of this crowd in my home and wondered how many guests have noticed my cheap imitations and possibly hidden scorn behind their smiles. Or maybe silently sighed, relieved that at least their walls aren't as sparse as mine. Which is ridiculous. They're my friends. What do they care?

Or do they?

Rather than basking in the beauty displayed on our host's walls for all of us to enjoy, I couldn't stop myself from comparing my walls to hers and imagining the décor gracing the homes of the other guests. I had taken the bait and was now dangling uncomfortably on comparison's hook, having lost a bit of the joy I had when I entered. I forgot that what's on the walls isn't nearly as important as what's taking place within the walls—the conversations, the laughter, the fights, the making up, the everyday stuff of relationship.

I looked around the room and couldn't help but wonder, *Am I alone?*

Did the man standing by the door think about the car he was driving when he parked and saw other cars nicer or junkier than his? Was the woman on the sofa worried about her outfit? Did she rifle through a closet only hours earlier, searching for the perfect clothes like my teen daughter does before meeting up with friends at the mall?

Could the journey through *her* closet be tracked, the way my daughter's can, by the clothes dropped across her floor? Like breadcrumbs left on a forest floor, discarded outfits attest to our mental anguish as we struggle to choose just the *right thing* to be okay.

Why would an outfit choice hijack our thoughts and prevent us from enjoying the people around us? How could a more-than-enough home suddenly become Less Than? Why do we—why do I—take the bait and make comparisons? It's crazy. And I know better.

THE THIEF OF JOY

The next day at lunch with my teen daughter and her friend Maddie, I described the scene from the night before.

Maddie offered up some honesty herself. "I totally get what you're talking about." She thought for a minute, then added, "In ballet, even though I've been dancing since I was three, I'm just not flexible. So when we stretch, I can't help but look at the girls that can stretch further than me and I want to be them. I want to be better than I am. And I wonder what it would be like if I could stretch like any one of the other girls." She paused to take a bite of her hamburger, then added, "It takes a lot of the joy away from what I love. I don't know why I do it."

I nodded and looked at my daughter, reading in her thoughts a wish not for flexibility but for the willowy thinness of her ballet friend.

Maddie had summed it up in a nutshell: "It takes a lot of the joy away from what I love."

Comparison surrounds us so thoroughly that we don't even realize how it's suffocating us, stealing our contentment. What we do see is that we're ever striving to measure up, concerned about falling short. If we do manage to come out ahead of the crowd, we struggle to enjoy it because we're fighting to hold on to our position or reach the next level.

We expect the Greater Than/Less Than jockeying for position in middle school. We expect it in the workplace, in sports, in academia. We're blindsided when it shows up as competitive parenting among friends. I find it even in the dresser drawer when I spy a pair of pants I wore before giving birth to five kids. The "someday" jeans that I hold out hope of wearing again hint at the need for a trip to the Goodwill drop-off—but can unexpectedly prompt a disappointing comparison between me and former me. As my mental scales pit me against my own expectations for myself, I feel the joy being sapped out of the moment. Then I remember that even when I wore those pants, I mourned for the hip clothes I had worn in college. So why waste precious time on something as ridiculous as old, too-tight pants?

Why? Because comparison is relentless. It casts a shadow over nearly every aspect of our modern lives: job, car, house, education, clothes, appearance, tweets/re-tweets, Pinterest pins, Facebook/Instagram Likes and Shares, YouTube views, even business cards.

What hold could a three-and-a-half-by-two-inch piece of thick paper have on anyone?

It's hard to explain, but something shifts in the air of a conference room when business cards are exchanged and titles enter the picture. The comparisons escalate as participants work in mentions of their degrees, their associations with certain institutions, their past athletic achievements, their well-placed connections. A little Ivy and NCAA can go a long way.

Comparison is the thief of joy.
—Theodore Roosevelt

The list of joy stealers goes on and on. The good news is that we can silence comparison when we learn to recognize its insidious invitation to self-obsession. Because really, that's what comparison does: it makes life all about me, how I measure up or fall short. And all that self-absorption consumes our mental energy and prevents us from enjoying life.

In my friend's house, I caught myself in that art moment, and I did one of the things that actually dispels comparison: I quickly forced a mental reboot and chose to be genuinely happy for my friend, our host. When it's not about me, I can appreciate her great taste and the beauty of what hangs on her walls. Then, adding a little *oomph* to my mental reboot, I reminded myself to consider the not-too-shabby aspects of our own home. Maybe the artwork on the wall next to my kitchen table is not professional, but there are a few objets d'art that are of great worth to me. Pencil sketches of a squiggly line elephant, a chair, a light bulb, a rectangle, and a cross, each drawn by my seven-year-old, have hung there for several months and never fail to make me smile. They remind me how quickly time flies. They take me back to the days when all my brood whiled away a day coloring, drawing, displaying—and going through the garbage can to see what treasure I might have mistaken for trash.

Such reminders of what I truly value help ground my thoughts in a saner perspective and break the grip of comparison.

Does comparison ever end? Who knows? Maybe I'll still be lured into dissatisfaction by looking at my former-me pants or art or house or kids or titles or status or (fill in the blank) when I'm eighty. I hope not. I hope that through honest discussion, we can encourage each other and find practical ways to tame comparison pressures. I think the solution begins with bringing unproductive thoughts into the light so each of us knows we are not alone in this struggle.

But before going further, I should probably introduce myself.

ONE OF THOSE MOMS

My name is Kay. I'm mother to five (mostly) delightful children. I'm a wife, a sister, and a daughter. I'm calendar challenged, organizationally impaired, a tiny bit forgetful, and according to my kids, I talk a lot. When we stopped to get gas the other day, I overheard one of them tell a carpooling friend, "Oh no. That lady just waved at my mom." After preparing her friend for the pending ordeal, she asked, "Do you need to be somewhere? Because we might be here a while." A sibling agreed, begging, "Mom, puh-leeeez don't talk!"

I am also a procrastinator. And I married a procrastinator. Together we are somewhat productivity challenged. There should be some sort of test required before two laid-back people get married. Not much gets done. Only on two occasions did we even leave the hospital with a child named. Three of our kids were "little guy" and "cute thing" for weeks on end before the blank on their birth certificate was filled. In fact, Jack was named by his sister as she was being dropped off at school after a week of people asking the baby's name. "Dad," she said while closing the car door, "his name is Jack David. I'm telling everyone that's his name." And that was it. Thank goodness someone can make a decision around here.

Most of our friends might consider us among the least likely household to be affected by comparison pressure—something about needing to be aware in order to compare. But comparison's far-ranging grasp captures even the oblivious.

I'm a former businesswoman. At some point before donating a majority, if not all, of my brain cells to certain children in multiple visits to Labor & Delivery at Baylor University Medical Center Dallas, I was numbers savvy. These days, given that fifth-grade math eats my lunch, I'm not sure how I ever worked in corporate finance. Jon assures me that I used to be smart. I ask him to remind me what I was like. And I try to remember the days when I could think complete thoughts, when I could start and finish a sentence without interruptions, when I could create multifunction, interdependent spreadsheets.

I no longer produce spreadsheets, but I still juggle complex planning in the form of the family schedule. Thank goodness the kids have become a bit more self-sufficient over the last couple of years, due to an experiment to rid our home of youth entitlement. The truth is, they're much better than I am at handling their lives anyway.

While the kids are nice enough to put up with me and my harebrained ideas, they still prefer that their identities be disguised in print. So here, in addition to Jon and me, is the cast of characters, ages seventeen to seven, at our house:

- Boxster. Named after a memorable conversation involving a Porsche and teen-induced car-envy. Needless to say, he does not drive a Porsche. And he no longer looks to things like cars to define his significance.
- Snopes. Known for her ability to spot any suspect actions, especially questionable driving patterns of her mother. I hope you enjoy her wise insights as much as I do.
- Barton. Though entering that season where attitude rules, the girl stays true to her go-to-girl namesake.
- Fury. He remains as passionate as ever, steering more and more toward positive ventures, including mentoring his tagalong, and arguably best friend, younger brother.
- Jack. Our sole real-named character, he has yet to shed his Mary Poppins's "practically perfect in every way" label, but we're sure the day is coming. Maybe that will become his pseudonym, Poppins. Until then, he's fine with Jack.

We have a regular home full of regular kids, all of whom I adore, even though the teen years really do push the envelope. So I'm not going to cut it as Mom Grand Supreme. Apparently I'm not alone in that assessment. The month of May provides plenty of confirmation.

For some reason schools pile everything into May: field trips, field days, birthday lunches (so all the summer birthday kids won't feel slighted), projects, Living History Day, end-of-year parties, end-of-year gifts. And e-mails, oh so many e-mails. E-mails about e-mails, asking if e-mails have even been seen. E-mails begging for a reply or at the very least acknowledgment.

At times like these I feel sorry for the room mom who has my child in her class.

In the midst of the craziness, a friend said to me, "I know this won't hurt your feelings, but, well, you know . . . you're one of those moms."

What? "One of those," huh?!

The truth is, my feelings were a tiny bit hurt as I wondered what "one of those" meant. I'm pretty sure I was falling short. I don't think "one of those" means organized or on top of things. And I'm fairly certain that it doesn't mean ahead of the game, mindful of grades, orderly, timely, prepared, or even aware. *(Field Day? What's that? And he needed a tie-dyed shirt . . . yesterday?)*

Maybe you're "one of those" along with me. Or maybe you're someone who amazingly has your life all together, wondering why the rest of us are chronically behind. Regardless of where we land, we aspire to live the "right" way, as if there is one. So we spend our lives observing, comparing, and judging. Then we strive. We view ourselves as Greater Than or Less Than according to the set standard—what we've done, where we've been, what we have or don't have, what we need to be okay—as it relates to those around us. We tend to view life as a race and use the good aspects of comparison to propel us forward, even sharpen our strengths. But somewhere along the way, we allow the negative aspects of comparison to rule as we make keeping up with the Joneses the benchmark of our contentment.

I expected (and often relished) the competitive challenge in school, in sports, in the workplace, so I didn't think much about it. But my eyes were forced open to comparison's insidious nature the moment I became a parent.

Maybe it had something to do with insecurity about my complete inadequacy in the area of parenthood. I don't know. But soon after the birth of my first child, I was hit by the relentless onslaught of pressure to get this "right." How and when my child slept, ate, and spent his awake time would set the course of his future life. So I started to look at what everyone else was doing, especially as it compared to what I wasn't doing.

Bombarded by differing "right" ways to do something, I felt a whole new world of comparison entering my sphere. Breast-feeding, organic baby food, playgroups (lots of playgroups), milestones, birthday parties, toddler sports, and Mother's Day Out programs—there was no end to the *should*. It was as if every new parent tried to justify her own choices by comparing them to those of others on a similar road. If only it had stopped at the infant stage, but things were just ramping up to the Olympic-level competition that parenting has become.

Never before had I experienced discontent at such unnerving levels. As I tried to breathe under the weight of all the pressure—especially since that pressure centered on something for which I cared more than I'd ever cared for anything else (my kids)—I searched to flush out the joy stealers. The more I searched, the more I realized that comparison was involved in almost every aspect of discontent.

Because it isn't exclusive to parenting.

I started to realize that comparison's sneaky little traps were set around every life corner. Even a morning stroller walk with neighbors wasn't safe from snares. It would beg each of us to compare the houses we passed to our own, producing internal longings rather than satisfaction. We all lived in perfectly lovely homes with food on tables situated on hardwood floors next to stocked shelves in kitchens with running water. So what if maybe I had to wash my dishes by hand since our 1940s bungalow had no dishwasher. Could I mentally reboot, be thankful for hot water, and find peace in the moment? Or would I give in to the pull of resenting our limited financial resources, wishing for a home with a second story or, at the very least, a built-in Maytag?

In today's culture, opportunities to compare run rampant.

I began to see comparison everywhere—in every arena and stage of life—driving our posts on social media, determining our educational choices, propelling our consumerism, filling our calendars with must-do events. It's like buying a car. Before making a purchase, we rarely notice the particular make and model on the road. But as soon as we begin driving, similar cars show up everywhere.

Now that I know its various makes and models, I see the peace-disrupting presence of it far and wide. Comparison, like an electric car, arrives silently on the scene and catches our attention through envy, "what ifs" and "if onlys," fair and not fair, measuring up, and striving for enough. Then it opens the doors and invites us in for a ride to the Land of Discontent.

Becoming a parent brought it to my attention.

Who knew a conversation with one of my kids would send us down the path toward a solution?

2

The Icebreaker

"Three" Little Words That Shift Our Focus

> **com·par·i·son** *noun* \ kəm-ˈper-ə-sən: the act
> of looking at things to see how they are
> similar or different.
>
> —Merriam-Webster

I tend to look at our kids' grades only two or three times a quarter. I avoid the information overload of the online grading system in part due to my very real technological issues. Last year, I'm sure due to user error, I never once saw a report or online grade for Snopes. I would hear parents talking about projects, tests, and so on and have no clue. Still, she lived to tell the tale. Which is probably another reason I don't over-involve myself. The kids are more than able to keep up with the work themselves. Still, I do try to look at marks at the end of a grading period just to be sure.

One fateful day, while driving my endless rounds of carpool and waiting for a bell to ring, I checked e-mail. Lo and behold, I found a message from school: "RE: Third Quarter Report Card."

I checked it out and found that Snopes had done just fine in this grading period, actually great as far as I was concerned. Jon and I aim to be satisfied with our kids' best, believing that "best" is measured differently for every child and takes a variety of things into account.

During this particular quarter, Snopes had weathered two ill-nesses that kept her out of school for seventeen days. Once she was well, I offered to help coordinate her work load, but a slightly tart "I can do it myself" remark left her on her own. My assumption that she would learn the power of a zero was completely disproved when I opened the quarter-end report card. All on her own, without any help from me, she had scored well. One or two grades were lower than she'd hoped but easy to bring up.

I passed my phone to Snopes, with the grade message open and a "you did this 100% on your own" praise, when she claimed shotgun for the ride home. As if on cue, one of her friends called to ask what Snopes had made on an exam and where her quarter finished. You never know what's behind such curiosity. I try to assume the best in-tentions, but still, it can be awkward. The conversation usually ends with some wind being sucked out of a certain child's sails.

I listened to the exchange that ended with Snopes saying, "That's great. Yeah, I'll see you tomorrow." After the call, Snopes looked at me, a bit dejected. "I studied so hard," she said. "I just don't get it. Why is my grade lower?" Her grade wasn't that low, and the fact that she had a good showing after missing so much school made it all the more in-credible. But life issues are rarely calculated into the bottom-line assessment. It's all about the numbers. "And why do people talk about grades in the first place?" she moaned.

"Did you do your best?" I asked.

"I tried really hard. Was it my best? I think so. I don't know." She's always honest.

"Well, it seemed to me you put your best foot forward."

"I don't know. Maybe." She thought for a minute, then continued, "Still, it makes me feel bad when someone asks. If my grade is good, I don't want to tell because I don't want the other person to feel bad. And if my grade is bad, I don't want to tell, for obvious reasons." Brushing a strand of hair aside, she added, "I'm happy with my grades until the comparing starts, then it's like I can't breathe." She paused and looked up. "Because I want to do better than everyone else. And if my grade is better, I like feeling smarter. But it never stops there. It's like I have to keep on being better or I'm worse than when I began."

Interesting.

"But when I score lower, I'm worse than everyone else," she admitted. "I really don't like that. It kind of confirms everything for me, that I am not as smart as everyone else and—well, it's gross."

Sitting in our well-traveled car, waiting for a brother who was taking his own sweet time getting out of school, the kid had just succinctly described the negative effects of comparison. We both chewed on her comments for a minute.

"I think you're right," I said. "That's kind of the way it works."

Of course, I couldn't stop there. I gave in to the irresistible mom urge to turn every conversation into a teachable moment. "That comparing stuff can be brutal," I said. "But I'm going to share with you three powerful words. They're way underused, but they breathe life into situations like these, for everyone involved."

The kid decided to go along with the inevitable mini life lecture and try to make it fun. She started to guess where I was headed. "All right. What are they? 'I don't care'?"

"No."

"Well, good. Because that's just rude." She paused, then tried again. " 'I love you'?"

"No."

"Yeah. That could be awkward." She thought for a moment. " 'Good for you'?" Her guess was seasoned with a bit of sass.

"No."

"Then what?"

"It's like 'Good for you' but without sarcasm."

"All right already." Clearly she was losing patience with the lecture.

"The words are 'I'm happy for you.' "

" 'I'm happy for you'?"

"Yep. That's it."

"Uhhh . . . That's four words, Mom."

No wonder the kids never want my help with their math homework! "Okay, so four words. They're still superpowerful."

I didn't tell her how hard it is to really mean those words, even for adults. Because while I want to be happy for people, I'm more likely to wish it were me getting whatever good things are coming their way. As in, "I wish *we* were going skiing" or "I wish *my* kid had gotten that job" or "I wish *I* could look that cute in skinny jeans" or "I wish *I* had it all together" or . . . well, you get the idea. The "wish it was me" mentality teases me with almost endless "if onlys." "If only I had . . ." "If only I could . . ." "If only I was . . ."

Are those few words—*I'm happy for you*—powerful enough to break us free from the downward pull of our self-absorption?

Yes, I'm convinced they are.

Snopes and I went on to talk about the fact that if you can for a

---

You're Not Alone

I find it challenging to stop my thoughts from wondering where I would be *if* . . . (fill in the blank). *What if I had continued working instead of going to law school?* I look at the people (who've all hit it big) at the job that I left in order to do it. And I wonder what my life would have been like if I had stayed and never gone back to school. Or *What if I had married my high school sweetheart? Would life be easier?* I don't mean to think that, but I do.

Right now I think, *If only we hadn't moved to San Diego, then our kids wouldn't be dealing with such rough social issues.* And I wonder if our decision to uproot them will have lasting negative effects. It's especially hard seeing how life is so good for the friends that we forced our kids to leave behind. It is a mental battle, almost every day.

—Cathy

---

moment get your eyes off yourself and actually celebrate someone else's work, achievement, talent—anything, even something as small as complimenting their shoes—it might make the person feel good, but it actually helps you.

"I'm happy for you" (if you mean it) breathes life into tense and uncomfortable situations. Being preoccupied with how we measure up personally leads to either pride or humiliation, whereas choosing to focus on and congratulate the other person lifts us both up.

It works with kids and grades. It works when a Facebook or Instagram post makes your stomach ache with envy or with disappointment. It works when vacation destinations dominate conversation. It works when your sibling gets an incredible gift for his birthday and all you get is a couple of shirts that your mother probably would have bought for you anyway. And it works even when your mailbox is stuffed with Christmas newsletters that confirm all the ways everyone else's home works so much better than yours.

"So," I told my daughter, "the gist is this: rather than count and compare, we can be happy for each other. Then the key—and arguably hardest part—is that we have to *mean it*."

She thought about it a minute, then replied, "I think that's a lot easier said than done."

"Probably," I agreed.

"But I'll try," she declared.

What?! I must admit her announcement to try took me by surprise. Was one of my offspring actually listening?

I hadn't really intended to put forth a challenge. I was just doing what I normally do: talk too much and think out loud, not sure if anything I say ever makes an impression. Snopes was so sweet to consider my babbling as a potential steppingstone toward contentment.

Being happy for someone activates a couple of letter changes in the word *comparison*. It removes *ri* and adds *si,* shifting the letters and our focus, moving our eyes off self to consider others. And in that shift—in saying, or at least thinking, *I'm happy for you*—we move from comparison to compassion.

com·pas·sion *noun* \ kəm-ˈpa-shən:
a feeling of wanting to help someone
who is sick, hungry, in trouble, etc.

Synonym—sympathy: the act or
capacity of entering into or sharing
the feelings or interests of another.
—Merriam-Webster

Sitting in the car, we pondered how "I'm happy for you" can almost instantly extinguish so many unsavory aspects of comparison. We thought about the way both peace and joy move within reach every time we live out those three (four) little words.

Easier said than done, though.

Honestly, in the midst of our uber-competitive society, I struggle to say those words. In fact, I tend to choke on them. It's hard to be happy for someone when I'm gasping for air just trying to keep up.

Which leads to the question, how can I make the switch from comparison to compassion?

CTRL-ALT-DELETE. THE REBOOT.

In order to break free from the grip of comparison, we need to clear room for a new way of thinking about ourselves, our friends, and those in the world around us. We need a mental reboot. I remember the days of earlier PC models, when the computer's capabilities were constrained to some extent by operator expertise, of which mine was limited. On countless occasions I'd find myself stuck in a circular operation, and the system would freeze. Often the only way out was a soft reboot. Pressing Ctrl-Alt-Delete at the same time would gently shut down and restart my computer, then present me with a clean slate to reapproach my work.

In the same way, a brain reboot can be helpful, especially in the midst of comparison stifling. Here's what it looks like.

Ctrl: Control the Thought Process by Pausing to Recognize the Problem

Curing comparison starts by being aware and by identifying the signs that it has infiltrated our thinking. As we learn to recognize the many ways it undermines our contentment, we are better positioned to deal with it effectively. Together, let's start calling out comparison and naming it for the problem it is.

Alt: Consider an Alternative Perspective

While I don't think comparison can be eradicated altogether, I'm convinced we can take steps to minimize its control over us. The first step centers on perspective adjustment. Considering an alternative perspective moves our eyes off ourselves and onto something more productive. But this isn't easy to do alone. As my family and I have opened our eyes to the problem and actively determined to fight against it, we have found freedom that inspires us not only to keep working but also to share what we've seen and learned—so we can walk the road together.

Delete: Eliminate Comparison—or at Least Tone It Down

Sure it would be nice to quit comparing completely, but we know that won't happen. We aren't victims, though. By taking steps in the right direction—refusing to let comparison rule our thoughts, dictate our mood, or send contentment into a tailspin—we can forge a new pattern of thought. All of which takes time, effort, and most of all awareness. In the pages ahead, I hope we can explore some ways to head down this new path together.

Just the other day, I heard Snopes reassure her sister who was heading for a team tryout. "You're stressed because you're making it about you and how you will stack up against everyone else. Stop for a minute. Look up and find someone next to you who is probably feeling the same pressure to perform. Just say something genuinely encouraging or nice to her, even something like 'You hit such a great serve. You're a really good player whether you make the team or not.' And you will feel better." She paused, then added, "It really works."

"Yeah, yeah. Doubtful," responded the stressed kid. "You sound like Mom."

She says it like I'm not there. As if I couldn't hear them talking. Sometimes I wonder if they realize I am a person. A person with ears. And feelings.

"Mom's right," Snopes encouragingly told her sister. "It actually does work. I've tried it."

I may have temporarily lost consciousness at hearing the words *Mom's right* spoken aloud. But when my brain function returned, I thought about what she said. About how forcing our thoughts away from self and looking to encourage someone else works.

If a teenage girl can grab hold of this truth, we all have hope.

This is where friends come in. Not as something against which we compare ourselves, but as another voice of sanity to join the conversation. Telling others about our comparison issues—bringing our personal shortcomings to light—feels risky. But it's key to gaining a more accurate perspective. That's why throughout this book you'll find stories and "You're Not Alone" and "Enough Already" sidebars contributed by my dear friends who've been nice enough to share their own struggles. While we may not be able to relate to every story, my hope is that these admissions will prompt all of us to consider and confront areas where comparison threatens to steal our joy.

A friend stopped me the other day to confess that when I'd shared with her my comparison discoveries, she really didn't feel like that was an issue for her. "Then I met some friends for lunch," she told me. "Within seconds of sitting down, I found myself looking at one of the women across the table and wishing I could drink a Frappuccino and still wear a size two like her. And I mentally chastised myself for only doing one circuit at the gym instead of two, because if I had done two, then maybe I'd be closer to being a size two. And I realized that even if I were the size I wanted to be, I would still want to be smaller or less gray or have fewer wrinkles or"—she gestured to indicate the list was endless—"and it was like the floodgates opened. I had no idea I could beat myself up over something as ridiculous as a coffee with friends."

I was grateful for her honesty. She reminded me that we're all in this together. No one is immune; no one is alone. And that sort of eye-opening experience is what I hope for all of us. As we talk about the many ways comparison lures our thoughts away from joy, we can also learn how to resist taking the bait.

Things like comparison parenting, body image, keeping up with the Joneses, obsession with busyness, one-upmanship, social media, and more lose their appeal when revealed for what they are—potential joy stealers. Together we'll be able to help one another reboot and focus on what really matters.

Putting a Face to the Name

Comparison just might be as old as time itself. In the story of creation, we find Adam and Eve, the world's first inhabitants, living in a garden known for its perfection. In beauty, provision, peace, safety—everything that one could hope for or imagine—the garden provided more than anyone could want. Only the fruit of one tree in the garden was off-limits.

Utterly content with all they had and enjoying their relationship with God and each other, Adam and Eve accepted that limitation—until Eve's eyes were opened to the fact that Someone else had something she didn't: the knowledge of good and evil. Enter comparison, in all its unsettling power, stage left.

Even with a perfect world at her disposal, Eve was lured by the idea that she lacked something when measured next to someone else. As she compared herself to God and His possession of the knowledge of good and evil, she contrasted her life with what it could be. The tree became a beacon, a neon-light temptation, to consider the standard she could never fully attain. In that moment, she misheard societal pressure (in the words of the tempter) as the voice of reason. And her perception of coming up short became more real than the sufficiency and perfect provision that surrounded her.

She decided to fix the situation by filling her perceived hole. Rather than basking in all the garden offered her, she stepped into the world of self-obsession as her focus shifted from the perfection she had enjoyed to this new deficit. And with her eyes on herself, she suddenly realized she had no clothes, a fact that had never been an issue before comparison entered the picture. Ashamed, she and Adam crafted makeshift outfits out of leaves, and they hid.

Most of us have known this story our entire lives. Only recently did I consider the fact that comparison was the lie that messed with Adam's and Eve's thoughts.

As Eve compared what *was* with what *could be,* her focus moved from simply living to being burdened by perceived inequalities. Contentment faded; discontentment accompanied by shame and blame flourished.

The story points to a universal truth: when comparison isn't involved, we are content. But once we start measuring our lives—against others, against what we could have, against what we think we should have—what we seem to lack takes center stage.

Before the new standard is set, we don't even know to be concerned. We're actually unaware. Comparison lurks in the shadows, completely out of play until someone or something reveals an inconsistency between what is and what "should" be. And with comparison come those tagalong sidekicks: performance and competition. All of which bullet-train us to the Land of Discontent.

For Eve it was a tree; for me it can happen via a Twitter text or even at the grocery store checkout. The promise of "better" tempts me in the form of "The Fifty Most Beautiful Kitchens." Magazine covers entice me to question how much I weigh, where I vacation (or don't vacation), how I entertain, and how my marriage stacks up. And I really don't want to be in those ugly pictures that black out faces and display ginormous cellulite-ridden derrières. Those pics tend to make us feel better. *At least I'm not that bad. Or am I?*

In the same way the garden inhabitants were satisfied until someone suggested something was missing, I'm content until my attention is drawn to something I didn't even know was absent from my life.

I'm happy with my kitchen, until an advertisement catches my attention and highlights the appliances with cool special features in a model home.

I love my yard, until the neighbors put in a swimming pool.

I'm healthy, but why can't I be svelte or waifish like her?

I've got great kids. But did they crawl before six months, walk before one, speak full sentences and learn to swim before two, play the piano by three? Because, you know, Mozart wrote his first piece at age five. And Einstein—well, who knows, but I'm sure he spoke four languages by age eight.

My boy can kick a soccer ball, but is he on the traveling club team?

My kids are smart, but are they TAG (talented and gifted)? National Merit Scholarship finalists? Princeton grads? Wall Street executives?

Our refrigerator is full of perfectly fine food. But is it organic? locally grown? gourmet? Pinterest perfect?

Where am I being left out? How am I sizing up? How do I compare?

According to the Centers for Disease Control, a sense of belonging and being connected are crucial to our mental health.[1] The longing to know we belong compels us to race after anything that offers to secure our feelings of importance and worth. But no matter the amount of stuff or accomplishments we accumulate, someone next to us has more.

No wonder depression, in which feelings of inadequacy play a major role, is on the rise.[2] According to the World Federation for Men-

You're Not Alone

For me, it's stuff. I'm content with so many things until I see my friends meeting each other at the pool. And I'm sad because I would love for my kids to be able to swim with all their friends . . . at the pool where we don't have a membership. Forget about my wonderful house, our car that works, living in a great school district, having a loving husband with a good job and pretty terrific kids. No, I want a membership to the pool. I need help! ☺

—Meredith

tal Health, "One out of ten people suffer from major depression and almost one out of five persons has suffered from this disorder during his (or her) lifetime. . . . By 2020, depression will be the second leading cause of world disability . . . and by 2030; it is expected to be the largest contributor to disease burden."[3]

Though I'm not claiming that comparison is solely to blame for the epidemic of depression, our chronic concern about how we measure up is surely not enriching our lives or relationships. Rather than appreciating people (or ourselves) for their own unique qualities, our thoughts race to assess whether ours are enough—or maybe better than theirs.

Andy Stanley, senior pastor at North Point Community Church, calls it living in the Land of Er:

> We are daily engaging in a lose-lose activity and we may not even realize how destructive it is. Being rich-er or smart-er or funny-er may feel like a short-term win, but for ourselves, our families, and our marriages, comparison is a game with no winners.[4]

Among other things, comparison has been famously described as "the thief of joy," "an act of violence against the self," and "the surest route to breeding jealousy."[5] Even Homer weighed in: "Nothing shall I, while sane, compare with a friend."

Can I be satisfied? Am I okay? Do I measure up?

The answer is yes. Yes, we can be satisfied. Yes, we are okay. And yes, we do measure up just fine.

But I will be able to get to *yes* only if I adjust my thoughts and the lenses through which I see the world around me—my perspective. I need to be wearing "garden glasses" that bring into focus sufficient provision rather than inequality. But with all the stuff going on around me, it can be hard to avoid what-about-them distractions.

In order to adjust my perspective prescription, I need to look at the "hows": *how* comparison plays with my thoughts and *how* to, practically speaking, do a mental reboot so I see beyond perceived inequalities to provision.

> **Sometimes your only available transportation is a leap of faith.**
> —Margaret Shepard

I was reminded about my perspective this morning when I got a tiny bit sidetracked. Sitting down with my cup of coffee before anyone else was awake, I opened my computer and somehow found myself perusing old pictures in iPhoto. Throwback Thursday filled my Saturday as I got lost on memory lane. I relished all the pics that memorialized silliness, stuffed animals, missing teeth, smiles, lame Halloween costumes, staged Christmas photos, and so much more.

My memory-lane stroll reminded me that good exists in the midst of life's challenges. It reminded me that we survived. We more than survived. We were stretched without breaking. We grew—even when many of the moments surrounding those pictures were filled with challenges, some of them severe. My stroll reminded me that friendships endure and that my outward appearance wasn't quite as questionable as I thought in the moment. The pics reminded me how utterly wasteful it is to wish away any moments or to let insecurities ruin them.

Tapping into provision perspective prompts me to consider that the worries and cares that seek to captivate my thoughts today aren't worth much attention. Maybe keeping in view the many life moments full of smiles and celebration can help me look at my friend's Instagram photo of her daughter's National Merit Scholarship and, instead of coveting that moment of joy for our family, genuinely celebrate that young lady's accomplishment. Maybe fixing my eyes on the beauty already present in my own life can help me be happy for folks around me—and mean it.

But provision perspective isn't as easy as it sounds.

Letting Go of Comparison

Looking at what we lack prevents us from noticing how sweet the world already is. But when we shift our focus from what could be to what actually is, we find extraordinary joy in our ordinary lives.

3

Beyond the Glimpse

How Taking the Long View
Changes Everything

> Everything has its wonders, even darkness
> and silence, and I learn, whatever state I may
> be in, therein to be content.
>
> —Helen Keller

M y neighbor stopped by yesterday to pick up her son, Sam, who loves to zip across the street and hang with my boys. After we traded small talk, I asked how she was doing.

"It's been a long day," she sighed. "Just one of those days when I feel behind, like I should be doing something and I'm not. But I keep reminding myself about the Glimpse."

"The Glimpse?" I asked.

"Yeah," she said. "You know. The Glimpse."

"Maybe?" My response begged for more details.

Both of our houses are situated in the middle of our block. To the east, our block dead-ends into a park. A very popular park where loads of action goes down. And, as she explained, where there are lots of opportunities for the Glimpse.

"Here's how it works," she started. "I stand in my front yard and look down at the park. Up pulls a Suburban. And out of the car descends a group of boys. They look about Sam's age; in fact, they might be Sam's friends. Or maybe not, because, honestly, I can't see that far. At the park is a huge inflatable bounce house and—and!—that mobile game company that sets up laser tag and whatever else they do. So I get all, like, worried, and my mind instantly goes to wondering if I know them and if I have been left out of something fun—or worse, if Sam has been left out."

Yes, I'm nodding. That's what we do.

"Then I catch myself," she continued, "and wonder why in the world I'm letting a Suburban with kids get me all mentally flustered. And I remind myself that the drop-off is a Glimpse. It's a moment in time that I'm letting play with my emotions as I compare myself to them."

She kept going, "Because the thing is, I wish I could throw a party like that. I wish my kid had that many friends. Then I think, 'No, I would do even more. I would take those boys to paintball and make us the *supercool* family.' But the truth is, that party at the park is a Glimpse, not a representation. Because those are just people. I have no idea what else is going on in their lives. Really, who knows? There could be great stuff; there could be hardship. But I can get so wrapped up in the Glimpse that I forget to see the people."

Then she added, "I hate the power of the Glimpse. So we're trying to stop it at our house. I'm really working on me *and* the kids. But I have to start with me. It's too hard to stay on top of them when I'm all distracted by Glimpses."

I loved her insight.

She's so right. What we see is often just a snapshot. Mistaking the Glimpse for reality generally leads us to either judge or covet. We land either on the feeling-Less-Than, wishing-it-were-me side of the scale or on the feeling-Better-Than side. Neither of which is beneficial for anyone involved.

I think about it a lot. One moment does not define a life.

I sometimes wonder what people think when they look at me. Do they think our family has it all together? Because we don't. We're regular people. I'm just an average gal, struggling with often-mind-numbing stress, mostly associated with my not-so-perfect kids whom I adore. If someone makes assumptions about us based on a Glimpse, any one of our moments, good or bad, would likely paint an inaccurate picture of our reality. And the same applies to me when I use the Glimpse as my measure of what's true about someone else.

Of course, this principle of the Glimpse also applies when I let a moment of loss or disappointment loom larger than it should and obstruct my perception of my own life. Can I look beyond the moment in order to see the big picture? Here's where provision perspective can help us gain ground against comparison pressure.

THE OVERLOOKED GIFTS OF LIFE

When the Joneses' grass is looking especially perfect, a good dose of gratitude helps us refocus and find the beauty in our own seemingly weed-riddled plots.

My grandmother used to frequently remind us that in every situation there is something for which we can be grateful. Of course my siblings and I just as frequently exchanged eye rolls at that little piece of advice. But now I see how wise she was. As a woman who lived through the Great Depression, whose first "home" was a room in the hospital where her husband worked, who lost the love of her life at the ripe old age of forty-six, she used gratitude to snap her out of almost any wallowing funk. I suspect the list of challenges she faced is much longer, since her generation never aired their struggles. She wanted us to do the same. Partly so she wouldn't have to listen to us complain or feel sorry for ourselves. Mostly so we could stand on solid ground. Gratitude does that.

It's hard to be grateful for, or to, anyone with my eyes on myself. But sometimes in the midst of challenge, especially when bumping up against something that glaringly represents an inequality (in the form of *this isn't what I hoped for* or *everyone else has something better*), landing on gratitude can be a challenge. I find myself in this battle for perspective often with my kids.

I tried to make this point recently at the orthodontist's office to an obstinate child who is frustrated by what seems to be an endless battle with an equally stubborn overbite. All of our kids have massive overbites and poor vision. So braces and glasses will be a part of life for each of them. The phrase *It's not fair* enters our conversation often. I told him, "This is a gift, you know."

"What?!"

"Seriously. You have no idea how much money we're saving you from future dental work. Even though you don't realize it, your braces are helping you when you eat, when you talk. In fact, maintaining good oral health even helps your heart. Not to mention braces will make your smile super nice."

Okay, so even I stopped listening to myself halfway through that little life lecture.

"Whatever." The kid pulled off a sigh-and-eye-roll combination. "You don't know how bad it is."

"Oh yes, I do," I assured him. Then for the umpteenth time I re-hashed my own orthodontic history: braces, rubber bands, headgear (not just one, but two headgears!), retainers (again plural). On more than one occasion, I found myself rummaging through Barwise Junior High's cafeteria trash in search of the oral appliance I'd accidentally thrown away—again.

Then, to underscore the "hardship" I've endured, I reminded him of my sight impairment and the lovely Coke-bottle glasses I wore until contacts entered the picture. At this point I heard groans from a couple of sisters perched close by, no doubt overwhelmed by visions of my youthful beauty.

"Listen, I know the pain, literally. I've actually walked in your shoes on this one." Then I added for good measure, "For it to be worth anyone's while, you have to be a participant in this effort. If you've de-cided to stop doing your part, you are free to get your braces off today.

I can't wear the rubber bands for you. So you're welcome to pay for braces yourself later when you're ready to commit. You're not a victim here. It's a gift."

A mumbled "Right" floats my way.

"A gift, I tell you." Now I've morphed into some ridiculous theatrical character.

"Okay, Mom. Braces are a gift. Nothing like a present that hurts and hinders sleep!"

The kid just can't see the wrapped-in-a-bow part. I'm sure I didn't either. In all honesty, I probably didn't appreciate my parents' sacrifice until we started putting braces on our own kids' teeth.

Even now I wonder how many of life's gifts I have labeled hardship and thus missed enjoying their benefits. How many times have my eyes been closed in self-pity or focused on what I thought I wanted. Good things exist in the midst of bad circumstances, if we're willing to look for them.

This is the truth I need to grab hold of when I'm enduring the whines, bandaging scraped feelings, mending broken hearts, navigating unpredictable emotional waves, weathering inevitable stresses—all the gifts that come with life. I need to remember the good when I'm in the midst of judgmental stares, whether they're mine in a mirror or coming from others in a crowd. But it can be hard. The moments might not seem like gifts in the heat of it, but on the other side, contentment enters the picture.

I celebrated another birthday last week. I didn't expect anything grand, but can't a girl hope for a little something on her special day? Sadly, my hope was in vain.

I could have kept my disappointment over unmet expectations to myself, but I didn't. Because in addition to my many other recovery issues, I'm also a founding member of Overtalkers Anonymous. So when I ran into some sweet friends I rarely see, including one whose birthday falls close to mine, I couldn't simply respond nicely when she asked, after sharing about her own happy day, "Did *you* do anything special?"

My curt response of "No!" left everyone looking rather surprised, even taken aback. I decided to run with this opportunity and air my disappointment. "Yeah, it would rank in the bottom five of all time for sure."

At this point, I'm sure everyone was searching for an exit. But caught up in the vortex of my pending rant, I continued, "Yes, if it hadn't been for Facebook love, my *special* day would have been a total bust. Besides a beautiful candle and some cookies from a couple of friends, my only gift was something I had bought for myself during the summer and put away in the closet for a special occasion." I did give the girls credit for remembering and presenting the "gift" to me.

You're Not Alone

After years of struggle, I finally realized and had to admit that gratitude is a discipline. It's one of those things that you want to feel it in order to do it. But often feelings don't precede an action.

—Connie

"They found it and gave it to me in the shopping bag from the store. And as if that wasn't bad enough, I begged one of the other kids to do something with me, even pleading with 'Pleeezzze? It's my birthday.' But he just looked at me, thought for a moment, and said 'Nah.' It was crushing."

If only I had chuckled and stopped there. I guess I took their polite smiles as an invitation to unload. Like a fire hydrant releasing water, I spewed about *all* my ills and mistreatments, not just from the day, but from frustrations pent up for weeks. From the kids' schools to family undercurrents, from the broken car door to someone blaring his horn at me on the way over—I shared it all in gross detail.

I e-mailed an apology the next morning.

"Oh my word! I'm so sorry that you had to endure me last night. I think I must be under stress (can I use that as an excuse?)!" These gals are my friends, so being honest about my struggles is fine. But drowning in them and pulling passersby down with me doesn't help anything. So I did what I should have done to begin with: sprinkled my frustrations with some gratitude seasoning.

"To set the record straight, I am blessed beyond imagination. Really I am—and grateful." Then I covered specific blessings that more than offset my ills. Because I am grateful. And I've never much cared about birthday gifts—the lack of which should've been more a sign of how well my family knows me rather than an oversight.

Being grateful in the midst of challenges goes a long way. Thinking about all I have for which to be grateful just might be the most power-packed mental reboot. I think of my grandmother and the countless times she reached for gratitude as a buoy to keep her head above water. She refused to let her life be defined by seasons of loss or disappointment. She took the long view, focusing on the provision that carried her through the pain or discomfort.

It's a time-honored solution for keeping life in perspective.

> **At the last, this is what will determine a fulfilling, meaningful life, a life that, behind all the facades, every one of us longs to live: gratitude for the blessings that expresses itself by becoming the blessing.**
>
> —Ann Voskamp, *One Thousand Gifts*

FINDING GOOD IN UNLIKELY PLACES

Before mothering, before corporate banking, I worked in various roles of Advance in the Office of the Vice President at the White House. The staff from Advance offices and Secret Service travel ahead of their respective principals to arrange the details of domestic and international meetings, public appearances, and other media-related events. It was the best job ever. I loved the variety, the intensity, the people, seeing the country and the world. A few trips stick out in my memory.

There was the Holiday Inn in Montana where our "rally" was in the hotel's *largest* room, which also housed an indoor swimming pool. I learned that day that trying to camouflage a pool with patriotic-colored balloons doesn't work too well. Chlorine eventually eats through the latex. And balloons popping as the Vice President of the United States steps behind the podium to deliver his speech sound a lot like gunshots. My stomach sank as the Secret Service scrambled and my boss radioed, "Who's bright idea was it to put balloons in a pool?!" Uh . . . that would be me.

In Warsaw, Poland, we were one of the first US delegations after the fall of the Berlin Wall to visit the new democracy. That trip created many memories, including lost luggage, food poisoning, ex-KGB counterparts not knowing quite how to respond to us (me), and accidentally running into and over Lech Walesa while racing to make the motorcade. Helping me up, he didn't quite know what to do with me, either. Especially as I stood, star-struck, face to face with a hero. I almost choked on my gum, which I shouldn't have been chewing in the first place. (Why they kept me on staff I still cannot imagine.) That trip was also memorable due to a very sobering, still difficult to think about, visit to Auschwitz with one of the leaders of the Jewish underground, who was gathering artifacts for the United States Holocaust Memorial Museum in Washington, DC. Even now, my stomach turns at the memory of revisiting historical atrocities with someone who had survived.

Then there was a 1992 visit to Johannesburg, South Africa, where, on a humanitarian effort, Mrs. Quayle led a delegation after the end of and during the transition from apartheid.

The tension was palpable in the staggeringly beautiful country. With First World infrastructure and Third World issues, the nation struggled to breathe on the brink of a new era. One man's fingerprints could be found on every milestone of hope.

Meetings of the Convention for a Democratic South Africa (CODESA) filled headlines, and the news programs begged attention from our US delegation. But our sole purpose was humanitarian. People groups were starving as grain rarely arrived at its destination due to hijackers. Our delegation was sent to assess the situation and provide assistance, not to weigh in on tense political talks. Everyone agreed that meeting with President de Klerk or Nelson Mandela would steal the focus from our purpose: to get food to starving people.

As we pursued our mission, I got to ever-so-briefly watch from the sidelines the pains of labor as this country fought to shed a history peppered with atrocity and give birth to the new vision the fingerprint man calmly, steadfastly, and peacefully promoted.

I never met him. But I felt him everywhere I went. Nelson Mandela led a country to look forward, with forgiveness. He kept his focus on what could be. He never appeared to wallow in the past. He didn't allow the wrongs he'd suffered to define his perspective. He could have. Especially as it related to the years he sat in prison, determined to stay the course of peace.

"Can I please go to Soweto?" I asked, pleading with my US Embassy counterpart to let me visit the famous township and home of Mandela.

"No," he replied emphatically. "It's just too dangerous."

"But I'd love to visit the hospital." Baragwanath Hospital was massive, overflowing with people seeking medical attention. Today it is the third largest hospital in the world. "We could help."

"No."

"Just a drive by, to check it out?" I toddler-begged. One thing you learn as an Advance person: if no is the answer, find another way. "You guys have the final decision, but just let me see if there's a way we can include a visit to the township."

"Fine." He gave in and arranged an escort.

I'll never forget my ride through Soweto. Though sometimes I wish I could.

What took hold in my memory wasn't the makeshift cardboard and tin homes, the filth, the smell, the masses and masses of people. It was the crying. It was the wailing. It was the smoldering remnants of tires that only hours earlier had been pried off the bodies they'd held prisoner before being lit on fire. It's hard to write. Harder to remember. Tears sting my eyes at the memories.

As I stared in horror and fought nausea, my embassy contact said, "This is why your team can't come here. It's not safe. The authorities are doing their best but can't be everywhere at one time."

> **True contentment is a thing as active**
> **as agriculture. It is the power of getting**
> **out of any situation all that there is in it.**
> **It is arduous and it is rare.**
> —G. K. Chesterton

In the midst of the makeshift shacks, permanent homes also dotted Soweto. Because before the hundreds of thousands of displaced people descended upon the township, homes had existed. As we drove, we passed a discreet house with a large wall covered in greenery. I noticed an armed guard at the driveway gate.

"What's that?" I asked the driver.

"Well, that's Nelson Mandela's home."

I couldn't believe it. There, surrounded by the tumult of Soweto,

You're Not Alone

My girls, Mary and Emma, recently went on a mission trip to Peru. The original plan was for a Saturday return, but the flight was canceled, rescheduled, then canceled again.

Soon after they finally boarded the plane in Lima on time for a midnight departure, the pilot announced another delay due to a broken windshield sensor. "Four hours later, we were allowed off the plane," Candie, the team leader, wrote in an e-mail, "We had half a cup of water, no sleep and some stress."

I was delighted when Mary (who turned sixteen while in Peru) messaged me over Facebook. "You must be tired," I wrote her when she told me what had happened.

"I am tired, but learning to be content and give thanks in all circumstances." And if that wasn't enough, she went on. "At least I am not working in a field on a mountaintop like some of the seven-year-olds I've met."

Gratitude. It's the secret sauce, the key, the thing that keeps our kids from being, well, brats. Keep them immersed in it by encouraging it when you can and enforcing it when you must. "One who is full loathes honey from the comb," Proverbs reminds us, "but to the hungry even what is bitter tastes sweet."

—Margie S.

understated, quiet, standing like an oasis in the midst of chaos, stood the home of the man who banked on hope.

Nelson Mandela committed to staying above the fray, refused to be a victim, and did what seemed impossible: he brought together people groups that for all intents and purposes hated each other. He encouraged them to look beyond the painful past, to focus on hope and the future. With a calm resolve he put one foot in front of the other. He never quit. He never asked anyone to do it for him. He never claimed that he was owed or deserving of something more. He served. He wasn't perfect. He was human. But it's hard to look at him without being moved by his resolve for a purpose much greater than himself.

Mandela lived a big-picture approach to life. Such an approach doesn't negate the difficult challenges or bank on momentary success. It weathers the inequalities, never allowing them to define the person. And he encouraged others to live the same way.

A hard task to accomplish if we're so preoccupied with the moment that we fail to look beyond the immediate and recognize that life is more than the Glimpse.

VISION CORRECTION

Every day we bump up against situations that present a clear choice: we can focus on ourselves and our successes or disappointments, or we can recognize that one slice of life does not define us or the people we encounter. But taking the long view, looking beyond the Glimpse, doesn't come naturally—at least, not for me.

It's like I need a pair of glasses—something snappy and cute—not to correct my vision exactly, but to remind me to broaden my perspective and to remember that life is about more than this one moment. To help me realize that the person next to me may be feeling just as rushed and stressed and inadequate, that there is more to a situation than meets the eye, that good can come out of it—whatever "it" might be—if we stop to view things from another angle.

I really needed those glasses in the Costco parking lot the other day.

"What do you think about lunch next week?" my friend Nancy asked. We had been catching up by phone while I drove north to the Costco in West Plano. "I can do—"

"Oh my word!" I cut her off. "Someone just took the parking spot I have been waiting for. Seriously, I was waiting with my blinker on the entire time that lady was loading her car and putting away the cart. I can't believe someone would pull in front of me."

"How rude!" Nancy commiserated.

"Can you believe?!" Then I shrugged it off. "Whatever. There's a guy coming up to his car next to that spot. I'll just wait for him." I went back to our conversation. "Okay, so next week . . ."

We kept talking while I waited. And waited. And waited. Slow Man had no clue, or didn't care, that someone was waiting to park. Out of the corner of my eye, I saw a car zooming up on my right. I looked over to give the driver my best oh-no-you-don't glare. But the driver, intent on the forward swoop, missed it.

"No way!" I told my friend. "A car on my right just swooped in! I can't believe how rude—" I cut myself short when I realized that car wasn't grabbing my spot. "Oh, never mind." I'm sure Nancy appreciated getting the play-by-play. "They're just taking the open space that's been sitting here the whole time on my left. My word! I can't believe I didn't see it."

She laughed.

"I'll just keep waiting. And talking to you." Really, I wasn't in a hurry.

Finally, Slow Man closed his trunk and walked his cart to the cart corral. As soon as he opened his door to climb into the car, another car turned into the aisle and sat facing me. The driver turned on her blinker to stake her claim to Slow Man's spot.

"You are not going to believe this!" I exclaimed. "Someone is trying to jump ahead of me for Slow Man's spot. I've been waiting here since he left the store." I stared in disbelief and started to inch forward to let her know that space was mine.

She just stared me down. And as soon as Slow Man began to back up, she wedged her car into the spot so I couldn't move forward.

"No way!" I gasped. "She nabbed my place! The audacity! *Oh my word!* I am so giving that lady a piece of my mind!"

"Are you sure?" Nancy asked, trying to help me gain perspective.

I ignored her. "You bet I am." Righteous indignation consumed me. "I've pulled in behind her and am waiting for her to get out of the car. Oh, she's getting out. Hold on." I put the phone in my lap and rolled down the passenger window.

Before I could get a word out, she yelled, "I was here first! I was waiting before you. You weren't even sitting there when I pulled up! This is *my* spot!" She added a little stomp for emphasis.

I couldn't believe it. "What are you talking about?" I spat back with all my middle school maturity. "I watched the guy walk out of the

52

store. I've been sitting here waiting long before you even *thought* about coming to Costco!"

She glared at me. "It's *my* spot. But if you must . . ." She motioned to get back in her car as if she were going to pull out and give me the spot.

"Oh no, you don't," I replied. "You just keep it. Happy day, Lady. *Hap-peee day!*" Mortified at my juvenile reaction, I remembered the phone in my lap. I picked it up and asked, "Did you hear all that?"

"Uh . . . yes," Nancy replied.

"I'm so embarrassed. I can't believe I said all that." To top it all off, there was an opening two spaces closer to the store's entrance. "Even worse, I'm now parked two spaces away from her. And now I have to walk into the store." Eek! "What if I see her? What will I say?"

Nancy (I'm glad she's a good friend) and I wrapped up our conversation, and I headed into the store, keeping my head low in order to avoid eye contact. I zipped through my list and had nearly made a clean escape when I ran into another friend. We stood chatting in front of the fresh flower section for quite a while, my hopes of a quick dash in and out vanquished.

As my friend talked, those flowers started calling my name. I couldn't shake the need to buy a bunch and put them on the parking-lot lady's windshield. I needed to apologize. My behavior was pitiful.

It was a parking space.

And she was a person.

Who knows how her day had gone? I needed some perspective and a reminder that our parking-spot war was a Glimpse, for both of us. Really, what difference would my walking a few extra feet make?

How hard would it have been for me to be gracious? kind? happy for her scoring a good spot?

Not hard.

And if I could have tapped into it, graciousness just might have met her where she needed it.

So I bought a bunch of flowers, then raced outside, hoping her car was still there. And it was! Thankful, I placed the flowers on her windshield, got back into my car, and drove away, wishing I had written a note of apology.

I'm not sure what I would have written, but I hope I could have said, "I'm sorry for my bad attitude and harsh words. You are worth so much more than a parking spot."

Because she is.

Letting Go of Comparison

Rather than be preoccupied with the moment, let's recognize that life is more than the Glimpse. A sense of lack accompanies shortsightedness. But when we consider the big picture and opt for thankfulness, we bring into focus abundance that might otherwise go unnoticed.

4

Do You See What I See?

Keeping Up Appearances
in an On-Display World

> This is one of the main reasons we struggle
> with insecurity: we're comparing our behind-
> the-scenes with everybody else's highlight reel.
>
> —Steven Furtick

*A*lthough comparison has called out to humans since the beginning of time, in recent years it seems to have become the loudest
voice in our lives. Growing up, I don't remember nearly as much pressure to perform at an early age as there is today. No one really cared
how old you were when you learned to read. Sure, some tracked ahead
of schedule. Whiz kids existed. But few parents made it a goal to raise
a whiz. For the most part they were content raising happy kids who
didn't draw undue attention to themselves.

Back in the day (no need to get specific on the decade, right?), no
one had access to videos in front of which a two-year-old could be

parked to learn how to read or speak other languages. Most of us were taught academic skills in school by teachers. We weren't racing after every opportunity in life. We weren't pitted against each other. Competition was a part of life, but it didn't define us. Comparison was around, especially in junior high and high school, but it didn't seem quite as all-consuming as it is now.

I'm so glad my mothering years began before grapes and cheese needed a skewer and plate presentation in order to be served. Thank goodness I could give a group of starving kids hot dogs warmed in a microwave. My paper plates and packaged chips of old don't stand a chance against today's organic-turkey sandwiches cut in shapes or numbers, accompanied by a locally grown fresh-vegetable medley perfectly arranged to resemble a clown face.

My heart goes out to young moms these days. And that's just the pressure at home, without even considering the challenges of living up to the other moms' school snacks and professional-level birthday cupcakes. Because everything has to be Martha Stewart worthy of a Pinterest share or, at the very least, an Instagram post that will garner wide acclaim.

Has social media changed everything? I love how one blogger addressed the issue, noting that ideally social media is a way to nurture relationships but that it has somehow become a prime venue for comparison:

> No one signs up for Facebook because they think, "I want to be jealous of my friends more often" or "I want to prove to everyone else that my life is better than theirs."

Those thoughts don't consciously cross our minds (at least, I hope not). But subconsciously we're engaging in a battle of one-upmanship like we're playing Words with Friends instead of sharing our lives with people.[1]

Social media offers so many wonderful opportunities for connecting. And I'm grateful. I get to be in touch with people I adore but rarely get to see. College roommates and cousins who live across the country, friends who share the same zip code but are in different life stages, and people with whom I might otherwise lose touch. In addition to maintaining old relationships, I've made new friends with people I've never met in person—genuine connections forged in the cyberverse.

One of the best aspects of social media is a Facebook birthday. We sink into and are encouraged by every single one of the heartfelt well-wishes on our birthday. Who knew Facebook could provide such a boost with a flood of *Happy Day*s that fill your page? Especially when our loved ones, on rare occasion, fall down on the job. (Smile.)

But as with any good thing, overindulgence and misuse can lead to some less-than-lovely experiences. Social media fuels our existing tendencies to compare. We script a pic to let friends know we're engaged, married, pregnant. We cover ourselves in memorabilia to let everyone know our kid has been accepted into a university—if it's a "good" one. We certainly wouldn't want to share the mediocre. (But wouldn't that be refreshing if we did?) We tweet about the new job. Instagram photos of our pets. Post stories about our beautiful, intelligent, and talented grandbabies. And on it goes.

I feel for young people today. Their daily lives are measured and arranged to best effect through marketing strategies, positioning, and perfect angles. They know all the tricks and gimmicks. When posing for a pic, try to be in the middle. If not, be sure to put your hand on your hip in order to give yourself a waist (a.k.a. the chicken wing pose). Practice a few times in the mirror at home to be sure you know your best angle. Use the pose in every pic, and you'll look good each time.

Through an incessant parade of pictures and announcements, we all get to compare our lives in real time. According to Shaun Dreisbach of *Glamour* magazine, "Approval seeking is intensified by the sheer amount of online exposure: 1.8 billion photos are uploaded and shared every day on Facebook, Instagram, Flickr, Snapchat, and WhatsApp alone." Further, women spend an average of four and a half hours a day online, two of which are devoted solely to social media.[2]

So young people join the photo barrage and get to compare their lives against friends' cool jobs, boyfriends, girlfriends, numbers of friends, social lives, adventures, relationships, engagements, babies. People get to "have fun" outdoing each other by creatively announcing things like the gender of their yet-unborn baby by using blue/pink icing in the center of cupcakes. Or better yet, film the release of balloons a short distance away at a "reveal party." Then wait for the "oohs" and "aahs" as pink or blue defines the day. Asking someone to marry you? Forget about a romantic dinner for two. Find a picturesque background, grab the phones (or hire a videographer) and film the entire thing. Bigger, better, louder, cooler, trendier, and wittier collectively equal happier.

Or do they?

Probably not so much.

Only on the outside.

The inside struggles to breathe.

We almost obligatorily, if not unwittingly, market ourselves, we brand our kids, we tweet witty quips and hope for re-tweets. We post our wisest or funniest musings, then gauge our likability by the number of Comments and Shares we grab along the way.

We peruse Pinterest. And click and save and share great ideas. Fun ideas. Helpful ideas that actually can make our lives easier. Hopeful ideas about dreamy spots we'd like to visit. Creative ideas for kitchens and fixtures and paint colors. Clever ideas and tips for everything we need to be more complete. And all these ideas to perfect every facet of our lives are pinned to neat and tidy bulletin boards of aspiration.

Then we do our best to keep everyone away from our home, lest they see the reality of our lives. If someone does drop by, she sure can't come upstairs or open the door to the laundry room where I stuffed

~~ Enough Already ~~

Somehow, it's not enough just to be pregnant anymore. Mommies-to-be want more: a clever, cutesy themed party, a decked out nursery, or one of a dozen other ideas pinned onto their inspiration boards. While these things can be fun and exciting for new parents, they're also more ways we all feel pressured to yet again keep up with everyone else.[3]

—Courtney Reissig

the hundred items left strewn across our floor and counters because, despite what my Pinterest account declares, I'm really not all that organized. Okay, not one bit organized.

In fact, let's just meet at the park or at a restaurant.

Because I really shouldn't have people over until I get my kitchen remodeled. Or at least until I hang new curtains—curtains that I didn't make myself in 1980. Okay, so I really didn't do that either; my friend Marcy made them for me because she could sew.

God bless Pinterest, Martha Stewart, the Barefoot Contessa, the Food Network, and every remodeling show on HGTV. You've helped

You're Not Alone

A few months ago, we decided to put in some long-awaited landscaping. As soon as we did, we noticed that the outside of our house could use a few updates. Of course it didn't stop there, since it never seems to be enough. We started some small updates inside. So I began perusing Pinterest, Houzz, discount sites, and every home-improvement magazine. All the "stuff" started to consume my thoughts. I justified it by my trying to get the best deal and something we would love forever. But in the process, I shoved my family and friends to the side. Even sitting next to them, I wasn't mentally present. I'm tired of *enough* and the way nothing ever is.

—Molly

us appreciate beauty. Thank you. You've given us great ideas. But you've also made it really hard to have people over. Maybe people are judging us, maybe not. But we most definitely judge ourselves and compare all the ways we struggle to measure up.

PLEASE TELL ME YOUR EYES WERE CLOSED

"I put some brownies in your refrigerator," my friend Alyssa informed me as we stood in my entryway. I had invited anyone who could to stay for lunch after our neighborhood gathering.

"You did?" Could she hear the hesitancy in my voice?

"I can't stay for lunch," she continued, "but I wanted to bring something for dessert for those who can." Then she added, as people crowded between us, "Thanks so much for inviting us."

I was touched by her gesture.

At least in the few seconds before my thoughts jumped to my re- frigerator and the possible horrors her kindness might have subjected her to.

The thing is, I grew up with people coming in and out of our house. It never mattered who or how many; my parents welcomed anyone and everyone brave enough to stop by for a visit or meal or rousing game of Ping-Pong. For my folks, hospitality didn't end with those who merely dropped by. I'm one of four kids, but we frequently had someone living with us who didn't share our last name.

My mother grew up the same way. Her childhood home had a screened-in back porch where guests who might have stayed longer than expected could pull out any one of the extra mattresses and spend the night. My grandmother loved to cook. She enjoyed even more feeding unexpected visitors, all of whom were treated like family. My grandmother always said, "You're welcome to anything we have. There's only one condition: if you want something, be sure to get it yourself. If you wait for someone to get it for you, you'll be waiting a long time."

I wonder if today's Giada-level standards would have affected her Crisco-infused, presentation-absent menu. Would she have been intimidated by what people might think? Or would she continue to feed the masses white-bread bologna sandwiches slathered in Miracle Whip, topped with a few pieces of bacon for good measure? Just thinking about it makes me miss those days. Her warm kitchen in all its very regular glory, with a soap opera or *The Price Is Right* blaring in the background, was the center of conversation, welcoming guests who sat at a kitchen table topped by a toaster that never saw a day inside any cabinet. Why put it away when you're just going to use it again? Hmm . . . I think I've heard that from my kids regarding their clothes on the floor. (Could it be hereditary?)

The priority of valuing people over presentation was picked up by my parents, who passed it on to me. Never once was our home perfect. But it was warm and welcoming. I guess that's why people kept coming. Whether five or fifty, it never mattered. My mother kept Pyrex pans of chicken enchiladas in the freezer *just in case.* So it's fair to say my hospitality training centered on caring for people, not being a slave to presentation. We focused on the big picture rather than trivial details, like a stray sock on the floor or nonmatching place settings or slightly charred main courses—so many things that, when combined,

could spontaneously combust into flames of overwhelming stress, fueled by the inevitable heightened awareness of what people *must* be
thinking.

I guess that history explains why I offered a spur-of-the-moment
lunch invitation to the women who gather each week in my home for
Bible study. For this particular occasion, recognizing that the topic on
our agenda might need more than its allotted time, I e-mailed everyone to stay for a sandwich lunch if they could. Nothing extravagant. I
had food I could pull from the freezer. Five or fifty, no worries. I'm laid
back.

Until Alyssa mentioned the fridge.

As my sweet friend told me about her brownie-gift kindness, my
stomach churned. I smiled my thanks on the outside, but on the inside
I fought the flight urge. I couldn't stop mentally inventorying our refrigerator shelves. I desperately wanted to excuse myself to look behind
those stainless-steel doors to see what she might have seen.

Oh my word, I thought, still smiling as if I didn't have a care in
the world. *Did she see the lettuce still wrapped in dishtowels?* I had
put extra washed leaves back in the fridge to have for a salad the next
day. But that might have been a week ago. Maybe two. I could only
imagine what *that* must look like. *Was it black? Did it smell? Was it
growing?*

If only my thoughts could stop at the lettuce. The towels rested on
top of chicken and potato soup still chilling in the pot in which it was
cooked. As did spaghetti in a different pot resting on a shelf above.
How long have those been in there? Have we even cooked since those
meals? It's not like we have endless pots.

Then there was the expired buttermilk, moldy cheese, grimy shelves, the inside of the refrigerator door cram-packed with all kinds of "goodies": a few open Cokes for some reason sporting straws, nibbled chocolate bars (Why eat it all at once when you can take a bite and put it back to enjoy later?), old salad dressings, open ketchup packets, week-old pizza (Who shoved that in the door?), a golf ball (stuff like that happens when one of your kids is a Future Hoarder of America). I could keep going, but suffice it to say that a surprise visitor to one's refrigerator can be a tiny bit unnerving.

I felt naked.

The reality of who I am rather than who I appear to be was crashing down.

What did she think? Did she notice all the mess? Sure the refrigerator was clean and shiny on the outside. But was she appalled by what she found when she opened the pristine doors and searched for a spot to place her gift? Should I mention I'd been meaning to clean out the fridge for a while and apologize for its condition? Or keep my cool and hope she didn't notice the ugly, smelly stuff lurking behind that immaculate exterior?

As I thought about my gut reaction to her seeing something that is normally hidden, I was struck by the similarity between that refrigerator and me.

Do You See What I See?

Life is full of doors we close to hide our less-than-ideal reality. We make the outside look good. We primp and curl, pluck and color. We take a dozen shots and select the best pic for posting—after some creative cropping and application of a flattering filter.

Because we think everyone else is looking our way, not always to appreciate but sometimes to judge. Life's a game where we position ourselves to appear in the right light, to be ahead, to win. And if not to win, at least to show well. So we shove our "regular" life behind closed doors in hopes that a shiny, well-groomed outside will divert attention.

We all have stuff we don't want people to see. For me, that stuff is primarily stacks and stacks of tasks that just never get done despite my good intentions, areas of life where I fall short of my own hopes. Yet because I do believe that caring about others is more important than caring about what others think, the fact that I stood in front of Alyssa's kind generosity and went to war with my thoughts surprised me. I've tried to free myself from how-do-I-look living because I find it so exhausting. I've gone through stages of life where the opinions of others held too much power. I thought I'd learned, the hard way, that handing over the keys to What-Others-Think can be dangerous.

But it seems I haven't completely escaped.

I guess I do care.

I don't want anyone to see my spoiled milk.

Even though I live most of my life in the Land of Regular—the land where milk expires, where old leftovers mold as they overstay their welcome, where clutter and wrappers infest cars, where closed doors hide overstuffed closets, and where the same load of laundry has been washed and forgotten three times—I can still feel vulnerable.

As my mind raced through the refrigerator shelves and all the things I was afraid my friend might see, I tried to remind myself that anyone who would bring brownies and put them in my fridge cares about me. Not about what I look like on the outside, but who I am on the inside—moldy cheese and all.

It's amazing how many things can race through a brain in a matter of seconds. As my mind sputtered to keep up, I fought to focus on the smiling woman in front of me. If she had noticed the mess, she didn't say anything, maybe because she's the kind of thoughtful person who brings brownies. Or maybe she just laughed it off.

Because her fridge is probably messy too.

So rather than let a messy refrigerator ruin my day, I sank into the fact that true joy resides in relationship. She didn't care about the state of my fridge; she cared about me.

I find it fascinating the way we can get tripped up by these joy stealers. As we chatted, the gal next to Alyssa joined in the conversation. I could almost see her thoughts churning as she realized someone had brought brownies and she hadn't. While I was thinking about my fridge, she was most likely handling her own mental battle as she thought, *Was I supposed to bring something? Because* she *did*. And the truth is, brownies or no brownies, organized fridge or messy, neither had anything to do with our perceptions of one another. But we all could have tricked ourselves into believing it did.

According to a recent study, thoughts like those consume a large part of our day, mostly during times of mental wandering. Harvard psychologists have discovered that "a human mind is a wandering mind, and a wandering mind is an unhappy mind." Matthew Killingsworth and Daniel Gilbert, the authors of the study, add that "the ability to think about what is not happening is a cognitive achievement that comes at an emotional cost."

Apparently, our minds wander 46.9 percent of the time.[4] Minds tend to wander the most while we're at work, in conversation, on the computer, and during a commute.[5] Why is a wandering mind unhappy? I'd suggest it's usually driven by comparison—thinking about the way things could, would, or should be.

And wandering thoughts can happen anywhere, anytime. My friend Lori told me,

I sit in a meeting and quickly go to comparison. I can worry that I won't share something nearly as impactful as someone else did in the room. Or I worry about how people will think of me when I contribute something to the meeting . . . was it really valuable, did I sound "less intelligent" than others in the room? . . . I think I have certain meetings that are triggers for me . . . if I'm the youngest in the room, or I'm one of very few females, etc. And all of these things can run through my head in a matter of seconds. The problem is, if I focus on comparison, then I am focusing on myself. Then I can quickly get defensive in the meeting instead of focusing on how I can contribute. It's just plain ugly, and I know it's not what God desires for me and my participation.

The answer to our mental self-obsession appears to be pulling the reins on those wandering thoughts and bringing our minds back to the people standing next to us. Relationship seems to be key to our search for peace. I can choose to simply accept the kindness without making it about me in some negative way.

AUTHENTICALLY IMPERFECT

So here's the troubling truth I'm beginning to realize: I struggle with comparison almost from the minute I get out of bed. I don't mean to, and I don't want to, but it has become so ingrained that it's hard to recognize when I've gone there yet again.

I need to remind myself that keeping up appearances is a never-ending struggle and start recognizing, be aware of, my battlegrounds, the areas where I'm most likely to worry about coming up short. Then mentally reboot. Something friends can often help us do.

Within minutes of my mental refrigerator-hyperventilation and regrouping, I was on my way to the living room and bumped into Jeannie coming out of our guest bath.

Again, I immediately felt my apparently fragile sense of self threaten to splinter.

For whatever reason, my youngest child has been choosing to bathe in the downstairs bathroom almost every night. The good? He takes care of his needs himself. The bad? He does the job, just not completely. The ugly? He consistently leaves behind a pile of clothes.

Like most little boys, he tends to be unaware of the mess he leaves in his wake, despite the best of intentions and repeated training. I don't understand it. How hard is it to put your clothes away after disrobing? Is it a guy thing? (See also: my bathroom hamper where a certain husband tends to place his clothes on the floor right next to the laundry cupboard rather than move maybe an inch farther to put them away. Hmm ...) No, my girls also have a tendency to deposit dirty clothes just outside, rather than inside, the hamper that is within inches of their own floored clothing. (Yes, it must be hereditary.)

Anyway, we've been having a small battle over our guest bath. I know and the child knows that clothes belong somewhere other than on the floor. But all too often that's where they take up residence.

So when Jeannie emerged from the bathroom, my mind raced to consider what might have been on the floor and whether or not a toilet had been flushed.

Of course, it works better to do the mental race *before* people arrive. I have such good intentions, but the road of my life has too many distracting off-ramps. Last week, I heard one mom laughing with another, "I just love that you can come to this house and find a pile of clothes behind the bathroom door—"

"Even one topped with skid-marked underwear," said her friend, finishing the sentence.

Nice.

> **Maybe it is our imperfections which make us so perfect for one another.**
> —Mr. Knightley, in the movie *Emma*

Standing in front of Jeannie, I tried to convince myself that surely the boy had taken care of his stuff. Raw from my refrigerator moment, I found myself worried about what she had seen and maybe what she would think about me.

Attempting to mask my concern, I started to greet her, "Hi—"

"Don't worry," she cut me off. "I took care of it."

"Oh. What was in there?" *Ugh. Apparently I'm batting 1000!*

"Just a few clothes and . . . some other stuff," she said reassuringly. Jeannie is a few years ahead of me in the game. She has grandchildren, so she can appreciate my spot in life. "I put it all in the bathtub. Then I pulled the curtain closed." She smiled. "That's what I always did when my mother-in-law showed up. I raced around the house, gathered everything, and threw it all in the bathtub. Then I would close the curtain."

"You're so sweet to do that." I laughingly breathed a sigh of relief, grateful for the absence of judgment. Then I added, "I love that you closed the curtain."

"Honey, that's what shower curtains are for." She smiled.

Our friend Melanie stopped when she heard our conversation. "Yeah," she said, "shower curtains and ovens and dryers." Then she added, "Just be sure to check the oven before you turn it on. I almost burned down my house once when I forgot that I had hidden all the stuff off my countertops in it."

I savored the moment, thankful for the gentle lesson. *Don't be so concerned about what people might think about you that you forget to engage with the person standing in front of you, who is most likely not judging you. No one expects perfection. Maybe from themselves, but certainly not from anyone else.*

I mentally lingered. Happy for authentic friends.

Apparently I'm not alone.

In that realization lies one of the truths that snuffs comparison. *We are not alone.*

"Why, when we know that there's no such thing as perfect, do most of us spend an incredible amount of time and energy trying to be everything to everyone?" asks Brené Brown in a recent CNN article. "Is it that we really admire perfection? No—the truth is that we are actually drawn to people who are real and down-to-earth. We love authenticity and we know that life is messy and imperfect."[6]

The truth is, I'm not one who normally cares about such things as a messy fridge. We have too many bodies in our family alone to actually be concerned about such things. But as my house filled with women, many of whom were relatively new acquaintances, my insecurities must have been ignited. So I had the chance to learn something I thought I already knew: when I'm less concerned with what people might think about me, my mind is freed up to realize I'm not nearly as messy or coming-up-short as I might think. And with those thoughts liberated from judgmental introspection, I can celebrate the fact that we're all in it together.

Letting Go of Comparison

Rather than worrying about what others think, let's consider the fact that people just like us are on the other side of those perceived thoughts—probably worried about what we're thinking of them.

5

Mirror, Mirror

The Beauty We're Completely Overlooking

> The aim of art is to represent not the
> outward appearance of things, but their
> inward significance.
>
> —Aristotle

W hen you stand up straight with your legs together, do the insides of your thighs touch or can you see light through them?"

Strange question.

One I had never before considered. One I've never really forgotten since.

"Huh?" I stared at my friend Claire, who had posed the question. We were just girls, sophomores in high school, chatting and laughing when the conversation veered in this strange direction.

"If you can see light, that means you're skinny," she explained.

She grabbed my arm and walked me over to the full-length mirror flanking the end of the boarding-school bathroom where we were brushing our teeth after breakfast. Perfect for a young girl to inspect herself before heading out to greet the day.

Claire and I stood in front of the mirror and compared.

Up to that point, I had never once considered whether or not my legs touched each other, let alone that this could determine my status. As I stood in front of that mirror, next to a genetically slender teenager, I held my breath. My self-esteem at risk, I said a silent prayer. *Please let there be light.* Ironic. Because in that moment, anything but light was involved.

By this time, a couple more girls had joined us in front of the mirror to check out their own thighs, wondering if in fact they were skinny. They wanted to see how we all compared. So we each stood in front of the mirror while everyone judged the reflections.

"Claire, yours for sure don't touch," said my friend Katie who had volunteered to judge rather than participate. I wondered if Katie was thankful to be away from the spotlight.

"Oh, and Kay . . ."

My heart filled my throat in front of that small crowd. I wondered why in the world I had submitted myself to this torture. I prepared myself for the envelope to be opened. And the winner is . . .

"Yours don't touch either."

Only then did I resolutely will myself to look in the mirror. The judges were right. Light. I could breathe. I was okay. Wow. To be standing next to beautiful Claire and be okay.

But I wasn't okay.

A new standard entered my world that day. My never-once-thought-about thighs moved front and center. Now not only did I have to look a certain way from the waist up, I also had to ensure that my thighs didn't touch. And for some reason, among all the other memories collected in my forty-some years of life, that mirror incident still stays fresh. A less-than-five-minute exchange seared a front-row spot in my thoughts.

Why?

Claire's question opened my eyes to a measurement—a quality I needed in order to be okay—I hadn't realized even existed.

Apparently Claire was ahead of her time. Recently "thigh gap" has taken over women's magazines and websites. *Shape* magazine reported that CoolSculpting, a medical technology procedure, received FDA approval for shaping services that fix the problem of touching thighs. So you, too, can have the gap—assuming you have the requisite fifteen hundred to four thousand dollars available in your budget.

> It's tempting to save and sign up for CoolSculpting. But there's something important to consider first: Before Photoshop changed society's perception of the female body, would you have ever noticed this so-called thigh gap, let alone coveted it? Make no mistake, this is a 100 percent fabricated look—seamlessly edited to perfection on screens, in print and now in doctors' offices.[1]

Isn't that interesting? "Before [fill in the blank] changed [your] perception . . . would you have ever noticed . . . let alone coveted?" It's a revealing question. And in this case, what's coveted isn't even real.

Women are comparing their legs to those of models who have been Photoshopped in magazines.

So often our supposed inadequacy is not even on the radar—we don't even think to be concerned—until someone or something reveals an inconsistency between what *is* and what "should" be. Suddenly, a new standard is set. Perception changes. Contentment is abandoned at the curb while we pursue the supposed standard of value. This is especially true when it comes to measures of physical beauty.

THAT'S WHY SLEEVES WERE INVENTED

The question of outward appearance stalks us at almost every turn, trapping men and women, young and old in almost endless iterations of self-examination. At dinner just the other night, one of the guys in our party of four couples asked, "Hey, did anyone see our waitress's arms?"

I managed to limit my response to a sigh.

"They were amazing," he reported with admiration. He was appreciating the results of her hard work displayed for all to see as she handed out the menus. "Chiseled," he added.

"Oh, I didn't see," said my girlfriend, sitting next to him.

"I asked her how she did it," he continued. "She said yoga."

"Yes. Yoga produces results," someone else chimed in.

"Oh, I think yoga is boring," another person said. Then they started talking about yoga, something about blocks on top of each other, the number of blocks they use, poses, and all kinds of things about which I had no clue. Then they moved on to the merits of boot camp, Cross-Fit, in-studio exercise, bike riding, triathlon training, and more.

The conversation isn't new. Years ago Dr. Kenneth Cooper made jogging vogue and ushered in the workout rage. Aerobic studios popped up everywhere, spurred by Jane Fonda and her sensual workout videos encouraging us to "feel the burn" so we could look like her.

But since all I do is walk or jog—mostly because it's outdoors, free, and doesn't require the ability to touch my toes—I didn't have much to add to our table's conversation. So I tossed out the only pertinent information I knew: "Arms are the rage right now."

They all gave me weird looks.

"Today it's arms. Yeah, they are what define beauty. Beauty and fitness, which I guess go hand in hand. Yesterday it was abs and lips. Tomorrow, who knows? It's a moving target."

Still no response. They just looked at each other. A few smiled at me awkwardly. And yet I kept going.

"Yeah, arms for women. And for guys toned calf muscles are huge. Apparently calf enhancement surgery is on the rise." The what-is-she-talking-about looks increased. But as usual, I continued. "Seriously. I read an article a few weeks ago that the 'in' body feature for women is arms and for guys, calves. They take fat from another part of their body and beef them up to look toned. Isn't that gross?"

They continued to look at me but offered no response. Jon squeezed my leg as a little "you can stop talking now" signal. My attempt to participate had turned into a Debbie Downer moment.

Still, the guy was right: our waitress did have nice arms. I wondered about the three other women sitting at our table. How did his comment hit them? Did it make them think about their own? Had the idea of an "arms race" planted itself in the minds of all who witnessed his admiration and endured my comments? Regular arms are *so* last summer. Did knowing this heighten their sense of vulnerability? Did it open the door to comparison? self-doubt?

> **I can still get my jeans on, for one reason:**
> **I wear forgiving pants. The world is too**
> **hard as it is, without letting your pants**
> **have an opinion on how you are doing.**
>
> —Anne Lamott

Personally, I was glad my shirt had sleeves.

Arms. Who would have thought they could set the bar for our self-worth?

At some point, all of us seem to find a reason to be dissatisfied with something about our physical appearance. Maybe it's not arms, but something leaves us feeling a bit Less Than as we look in the mirror.

THE HIGH COST OF REFLECTION OBSESSION

Toned arms, six-pack abdomens, wrinkle-free brows, youthful glow, straight hair, curly hair—measures for how to achieve the ideal look abound, trying to sell us the belief that if we could just fix that one thing, happiness would be at hand.

Though we often associate it with teenage girls, obsession with outward appearance reaches beyond, boundaries of age, gender, and even culture, presenting itself in the most remote regions of the world in body piercings, face painting, ear stretching, and other forms of body modification. All of which highlight the reality that ideals of human beauty are not fixed. And yet still we pursue the perfect image to present to the world. The topic of dissatisfaction with our bodies pervades everyday conversation, sowing seeds of discontent that may be landing and sprouting in places we never intended.

Last week I went to lunch with a couple of friends. When the waiter showed up, one woman told him, "Nothing for me. Only water today."

Having just ordered crab cakes, a salad, and sweet tea, I couldn't help but ask, "Really?" She's the one who had invited us to lunch, so I was a bit surprised.

"Oh, I'm on a juice fast."

Unfazed, our other friend commented, "Oh, you're going to love it. How long are you doing it?"

"This time two weeks," she replied. "You know, the beach is always around the corner."

I looked at her. Then at my other friend. Both women could accurately be described as waifish—and as mothers of teen/tween daughters who were surely absorbing the messages their moms were unintentionally sending: "You can never be too thin." "If you think you're fat, don't eat." "If in doubt, cleanse." My heart was troubled.

With all the outward-appearance pressures that daily assault us and our daughters—and sons—are we thinking about the message our actions send our kids? Because they are watching and learning from us, even when we'd really rather they didn't. It might not be a cleanse for me, but it's something.

Not long ago while driving carpool, I sat at a stop sign, waiting to go straight across Hillcrest. My version of waiting meant that I had already rolled into the intersection a bit, anticipating a quick cross. But before I could do it, a car obviously needed to turn in the direction I planned to go. So I decided to make a right turn to get out of that car's way. Then I changed my mind midturn, thinking, after all, that maybe I could get across before it. My indecision resulted in my blocking the intersection completely.

"What are you doing?!" my daughter screeched from the backseat.

"Well, I thought I could go straight by turning." Flustered, I tried to figure a way out of the jam resulting from my indecision. "But I'm messing it all up." Nothing like stating the obvious. "Okay, so this is pretty much how *not* to drive."

"Good to know, Mrs. Wyma," said my daughter's friend Maddie. She seems to always be along for the ride when I'm blundering. "You can never have enough examples of how *not* to do something."

What can you do but laugh . . . and love. I've heard it covers a multitude of blunders.

My point is, the kids are watching and listening, learning from us how to define what a normal life looks like. We may think the danger lies in the messages sent through music, media, and advertising, but our kids are continually digesting our casual comments to friends over dinner, overheard phone conversations, and daily actions that solidify the message that worth is defined by outward appearances.

Erin Schreyer, life coach and speaker, shared with me the following:

> I struggled after becoming a resident of the Lone Star State. Here I am in the Bible Belt, and yet instead of embracing how I was made, I got caught up in the comparison game. Rarely, if ever, did I "win" the comparison in my mind. And I realized that my thoughts and actions could influence my daughter, my sweet seven-year-old, who is taller and "bigger" than most of the other little girls her age.
>
> She asks me, "Am I fat? The other girls on the playground say I'm fat."
>
> I respond, "No. You're beautiful. You're healthy and strong and made very intentionally by God. He doesn't make mistakes. He made you just the way you're supposed to be."
>
> Television, social media, billboards, magazines, music, and virtually most of the retail industry support an unhealthy myth that not only ties a woman's value to her appearance but also defines an unrealistic image of what "pretty" even is. Girls can easily internalize that pressure.
>
> Of course I want to look my best, and I absolutely want to be healthy . . . but I need to challenge myself to consider if my choices are for my health or for my ego.

For the sake of our sanity, for the sake of the next generation, maybe we all need to adjust our mirrors.

A MIRROR WITH A VIEW

Most of us have a love/hate relationship with mirrors. Some days, in the right lighting, we can walk away confident. On other days we see only the flaws, glaring like a red flashing light to warn us that all passersby will see them too. But what we see looking back at us from the metallic-coated piece of glass may not be an accurate representation of what actually is.

To prove this point, Dove, the beauty company famed for its feel-

You're Not Alone

As funny as it sounds, I've had seasons of comparison. When I was in high school, I compared my hair and skin. My hair was (and is) naturally curly, doesn't look cute wet, and I had a horrible complexion. I always felt like the ugly duckling, except I was thin and looked cute (I thought) in clothes. I used to say, "Well, at least I have that going for me."

My single season of feeling like I had it all was from college through early marriage. I got a straightener, my face cleared up, I was still thin and cute, and I was married to a great guy (still am). I was awesome! Even after my four kids (three pregnancies, you do the math), I felt pretty good about myself.

Then in May 2010, I was diagnosed with celiac disease,

good campaigns, gathered a group of women and invited them to a function where they each met a stranger and were asked to get to know that person. The next day, the women were escorted to a warehouse where they were asked to describe themselves to a different person they had never met, who sat at a drafting board on the other side of a curtain. The person asked each woman questions about herself. "Tell me about your hair . . . your chin . . . your jaw," and so on. The women responded with comments along the lines of "My mom told me I have a big jaw," "I have a fat, rounder face," "I would say I have a pretty big forehead."

which means I can't eat wheat products. Because I had gone undiagnosed for many years, I had lost weight since I wasn't absorbing nutrients. Therefore, I was sick but skinny! When I stopped eating gluten, my body started absorbing again, and—you guessed it—I gained weight. This has been really difficult for me.

I compare myself to my former "me" and to others my age who, for the most part, seem to be sitting somewhere in their goal weight. Not me. It's so frustrating and upsetting at times.

My husband, for the record, could not be greater about it. I know he loves me at any size. . . . I know I need to (a) get content or (b) do something about it. I am stuck and frustrated. Comparison makes it worse and I know it.

—Stephanie

It didn't take long for them to realize that the person on the other side of the curtain was drawing their portrait. What the women didn't know was that the individual asking the questions was an FBI-trained forensic artist.

After chatting with the women, the artist thanked them, and they left. Then the strangers they'd met the previous day were brought in and asked the same questions about the women. The artist drew a second set of sketches based on the strangers' answers.

Interestingly enough, the self-described sketches bore little resemblance to the women. And in every case, the strangers' descriptions resulted in a more favorable, more accurate representation of the women.

The resulting video, titled *Dove Real Beauty Sketches,* garnered almost twenty million views within its first week of release. A little more than a year later, over sixty-three million viewers had tuned in to see the convicting results. Watching the women process the two sketches moves each viewer to consider that maybe we, too, see ourselves in a light less favorable than what is actually true.

One woman, visibly moved by comparing her two sketches, said, "I should be more grateful of my natural beauty. It impacts the choices and friends that we make, the jobs we apply for, how we treat our children. . . . It couldn't be more critical to our happiness."

Then another said, "We spend a lot of time . . . analyzing and trying to fix the things that aren't quite right, and we should spend more time appreciating the things we do like."[2]

We come to the mirror with a set of expectations, fears, preconceived ideas, hopes, dread—so many emotions. Older men inspect for hair loss; younger men dread hair arrival. Older women try to hide wrinkles, splotches, puffiness; younger women want the flawless skin of the (airbrushed) cover model. And that's just from the neck up. Who wants to see the whole thing?!

Each of us carries a mental mirror, a reflection of preconceived, often skewed ideas about how we look and how we should look. Our mental mirrors more often than not tell us lies that send a crushing blow to our contentment.

How is it that we give the mirror such power over us? In reality, it's nothing more than a tool that functions in accordance with the law of reflection, which

> says that when a ray of light hits a surface, it bounces in a certain way, like a tennis ball thrown against a wall. . . .
>
> With [a mirror's] smooth surface, light reflects without disturbing the incoming image. . . . That concept raises an interesting question: If mirrors preserve the images that hit them, why do they turn left into right and vice versa? Why not up and down? The truth is that a mirror doesn't really reverse left and right. What mirrors switch is front and back, like a printing press or a rubber stamp. Imagine writing something on a sheet of paper in dark pen and then holding it up to a mirror. It looks backward, but it also looks the same as if you held it up to a lamp and looked at it from behind. Your mirror image is a light-print of you, not a reflection of you from the mirror's perspective.[3]

∼ Enough Already ∼

Recently I had a mammogram, which is always a *smashing* good time. I am so grateful for the many ways that Solis Women's Health goes out of their way to make this potentially fearful time as pleasant as possible.

Before leaving I complimented the staff on how they made it easy to be transparent and not feel self-conscious about standing there letting it all hang out. They created the atmosphere of authenticity that allowed women to accept the bodies they were housed in. As I drove away, I reflected on how much easier it is to simply be "real."

However, that night my Cinderella joy bubble turned back into a pumpkin when I attended a party for my husband's work in my new and lovely size 12 outfit. In looking around, I quickly realized that none of the other women had gotten the "Size 12 is normal" memo. They paraded around in their perfectly toned size 4 bodies, revealing beautifully sculpted arms while I had mine carefully covered.

Sitting there with my arms crossed over my *not-so-flat* tummy, since I couldn't use the excuse of "Well, I just had a baby," I flashed back on my growing up years. I'll confess that I, too, laughed at times when a teacher's arms would sway as she wrote on the chalkboard and I vowed that I would *never* let that happen to mine. I remembered the day when I was in my fifties and thought there was a tsunami coming but realized it was my arms flapping in the pool. Much as I exercised and willed my arms to obey, they now seemed to have a life of their own. Good-bye to sleeveless dresses and hello to pride as I layered up, sweating away in the Texas summer heat.

Fortunately, my sixties brought freedom for me. "At my age I have a right to look whatever way I do," I told myself. "I am not young and I don't need to pretend to be!" I could even laugh with my grandson when he played with my arm as I read to him. I looked down at him and smiled, and he said, "Grandma, your arm is kind of jiggly." Yep, it's jiggly. Well put, sweetie!

But sitting at this party, I found nothing funny about my "jiggly" body. The morning's transparency at Solis was but a faint memory until the moms at the party began to lament the challenges of raising children. Since my children were raised, I had grandchildren, had worked with children for forty-three years, and yes, even had written books on parenting, they looked at me through a new lens, as did I. Suddenly I had value! It didn't matter what I looked like; it mattered that I could help them.

Reflecting upon this later, I realized that I had fallen into the same trap I have long counseled others to avoid! I lost perspective on what was really important.

My professional life has been committed to helping each child, teen, teacher, and parent see their individual giftedness. We are uniquely gifted by God for His purpose. When we rest in His assurance, happy with who we are, we are freed to say to others, "I am happy for you"—and mean it.

—Jody Capehart

I love the concept of a "light-print" because that just might be the answer to my love/hate relationship with the mirror.

What if I switched mirrors? What if I considered my true reflection to be found in the way God sees me, not in how I see myself? What if I allowed my reflection to be informed by God's light rather than the shifting light of societal values? Isn't the message of each individual's innate worth the one I really want to pass on to my kids? the one I should consider for myself?

My children each entered life with a unique personality, on display almost the minute they were born. (Exhibit 1: a certain baby who came into the world on her terms after fourteen hours of hard labor continues to be nearly immune to the expectations of others.) So, too, their body types seem predetermined to some extent. I've had to cajole and convince one of them that she's 100 percent fine the way she is.

"Sweetheart, none of us look the same," I struggled to explain. "Let me ask you a question."

"Okay," she said.

"Do you think I'm fat?" Okay, so I'm just going to say, that's a scary question to float. My perception would tempt my thoughts to land on a pathetic yes. But I really do know better.

"No," she said honestly. "You're not fat."

"All right," I nodded. "Now stand me next to Mrs. Cash. Just for a minute think about her. Next to her, am I fat?"

She didn't say anything. Maybe afraid to hurt my feelings.

"Honey, Mrs. Cash and I have totally different bodies." She is naturally thin. Her build is totally different from mine. "Her thinness has nothing to do with me. Her body type doesn't affect whether or not I'm thin or fat. But sometimes we get stuck believing that a particular standard determines whether or not we are okay. And more times than not, that standard has nothing to do with us."

She was thinking and digesting. I was wondering if any of it would stick. It's hard being a young girl, especially in an era when people airbrush their own selfies to create higher cheekbones or thinner legs.

"You yourself said that I'm not fat," I reminded her. "And neither are you."

What if, as one of the women in the Dove experiment said, we were to focus not on trying to fix the things that aren't quite right but on appreciating the things we do have going for us?

Glamour magazine recently conducted a follow-up to a survey from thirty years ago on how women feel about their bodies. No surprise: the results revealed that women feel worse about themselves today. And the negative feelings seep into all areas of our lives. Jesse Fox, PhD, an Ohio State University professor who assisted with the survey, observed,

> What's so toxic about all of this . . . is that for many women,
> weight and body shape are tethered to who they fundamentally
> are as a person—tied to their success at work, in relationships,
> everything. Which means, if you feel bad about your body, you
> feel bad about who you are at the core.[4]

What can we do? According to the experts consulted for the *Glamour* article, we should interact with the social-media world with eyes open: "When you log off, do you feel worse than when you logged on? If so, it's time to cut back." We can exercise, which women who do like their bodies say is more effective than crash dieting at dispelling negative body image. We can rewire our brains by appreciating ourselves: "Try out a positive word for yourself; think it—and say it."[5]

But mostly, we can stop comparing.

Newsflash! The survey revealed that women who are content with their bodies didn't compare themselves to others. To quit the comparison cycle, the same article quotes the suggestions of Lara Pence, a body image specialist at the Renfrew Center:

> "Think of great qualities about yourself that have nothing to
> do with your body—say, everyone laughs at your jokes." Now,
> every time you hear yourself starting in with "I wish I had her
> legs," tell yourself, "Stop!" Then try something like, "Good for
> her that she's got nice legs. And lucky for me that I have (insert
> one of your go-to qualities)." Sounds silly—but Pence swears it
> helps.[6]

What if getting our eyes off our own misconceptions about our bodies could help us recognize opportunities to help others be happier about themselves?

A few years ago, I dragged my crew into one of our favorite sandwich shops for lunch. As we walked in, the first thing I noticed was a morbidly obese woman at the counter ordering her meal.

Anyone with little children understands that, without warning, unfortunate/uncensored/not-intentionally malicious things can come out of their mouths. I said a quick prayer that my kids would keep any commentary to themselves.

Right then I felt a tug on my skirt.

"Mom!" loud-whispered my sweet, incredibly sensitive five-year-old Snopes. "*Mom!* Look at that lady over there!" Arm outstretched, she emphatically pointed to the overweight woman at the counter.

I couldn't believe that *this*—my ever-encouraging, bright-side—child, of all my kids, would be the one to inform the diners that a large person was in our midst.

"Sshhh! Don't say a word!" I hissed.

"But, Mom. Can I go say something to her?"

"No!" I cringed, slightly disappointed.

Dejected and obediently falling into line, she quietly informed me, "I just wanted to tell her how pretty she looks."

There are some moments when I would like to moonwalk to the closest exit or rewind and get a second chance. This is one that I will never forget. I told her she could absolutely go to the woman.

She scootched her way through the line and up to the woman. Now she tugged on *her* skirt.

"Excuse me, ma'am," said the sweet little voice.

The woman looked around, then down. You could almost see her physically and emotionally brace herself.

"Excuse me."

"Yes?" the lady sighed. "May I help you?"

"I just wanted to tell you how beautiful you look. I think your skirt looks so pretty with your boots."

She was right. The skirt did look great with those boots. The woman choked out a "thank you," and my daughter skipped back to us, having matter-of-factly done what she would have for anyone of any size, any age, any color, with not one thought of herself.

We ordered and sat down to wait for and eat our meals, our focus having moved on.

Then I felt a hand on my shoulder. The woman had stopped by our table on her way out. With tears in her eyes, she said to me, "You have no idea what your daughter did for me today. Thank you."

Snopes's kind words had caressed the wounded soul of this woman who felt constantly judged, not only by others but most likely herself. Such a powerful reminder to watch for the beauty that is always present—in others and in ourselves, guys and girls.

Letting Go of Comparison

Contentment comes when we choose to see the immeasurable, incomparable beauty of each human, including the one in the mirror.

6

The Dangers of Yardstick Living

Why We'll Never Measure Up . . .
and Really Don't Need To

> Many people lose the small joys in hope for
> the big happiness.
>
> —Pearl S. Buck

*A*s if his very existence depended upon it, a determined six-year-old Jack stepped up to the wall and stretched his spine to its fullest extent. A measuring stick reached up the wall's corner edge, capping off at fifty-five inches. At the forty-eight-inch mark, a bold arrow labeled *This High* marked the threshold that would determine the child's fate.

We held our breath and awaited the results. I've never seen him stand so tall.

It was Day Five of our staycation, and I was doing my best to make "the worst spring break ever" a little better.

Rarely have we worried about travel plans, packing, traffic patterns, or catching a flight because we usually don't go anywhere for spring break. Our traditional destination location is home. When the kids were little, they didn't notice. Not so anymore.

"Do you think I'll ever learn how to snowboard?" Fury asked last week, thinking about all the fun his friends had been talking about at school. (No need to point out his question carried with it a hint of comparing his situation to "everyone else" with the conclusion: *My friends are doing it; I'm not. All is not right in the world.*)

"Yes, honey," I cheerfully replied. "Of course you will." I hoped my prediction would be true. But vacations with seven people, seven plane tickets, seven lift tickets, and accommodations for multiple days can set a family back. It's not that we don't want to, but for today, our budget is allocated elsewhere.

I remember skiing in college with my buddies and feeling sorry for the poor soul whose first introduction to the mountains occurred as an adult. Now I'm resigning myself to the fact that the "poor soul" will more than likely be my kids. I'm holding out hope that either Jon or I can take individual weekend trips here and there, a kid or two in tow, so they can broaden their horizons.

Meanwhile, thanks to the wonders of Facebook, Instagram, and Twitter, I see almost everyone we know "making memories," and I worry. Our oldest will soon graduate. When it comes time to leave home, what memories will he, or any of them, take along? (Now I'm doing it!)

We started this most recent vacation with a bang. Actually a box of donuts. What better way to start a vacation than with frosting-coated carbs and saturated fat? We settled in around our kitchen table where I, easing into spring break excitement, had started a puzzle. We built that puzzle three times. Of course all but one of the kids abandoned me mid-Take 1, opting instead for the television.

The vacation exhilaration continued with reruns of *The Middle* and even more thrilling shows like *Man v. Food* and *My Cat from Hell*. Apparently, there's no topic cable television fails to address. Trouble with your cat? There's a guy for that. He brings peace and cat love for all. (Note: we don't even have a cat.)

At this point my attitude might have needed a slight adjustment.

Donuts, puzzle, television. That's how we started our week o' fun, and things went somewhat downhill from there. I'm not sure what I was thinking, but I piled it all in. Haircuts, shoe shopping, closet cleaning, the dentist, the orthodontist. I even went so far as to schedule the older kids for aptitude testing. The words "This is the worst spring break *ever*!" might have tumbled from one of their mouths.

I was tempted to agree.

We went to the park. We went to the movies. We Grouponed, which is how we ended up with Jack standing in front of an arrow that would determine his fate, willing himself to grow a quarter inch so he could make the mark.

Just a few minutes earlier we'd entered King Spa & Sauna with Groupon in hand, pinning our hopes on an indoor water-park adventure. As first-time visitors, we found a facility that boasted cleanliness, friendliness, and a heavy emphasis on safety. Whistle-toting lifeguards ensured every child adhered to the rules. No running. No rough-housing. No kids under forty-eight inches allowed in the water without a life vest, regardless of aquatic skill.

Since our older two were at the aptitude testing center and Barton was with a friend, I had only Jack and Fury (who had brought a neighbor friend) with me. Even though inclusion is a rule in our house, it warms my heart that these bigger boys genuinely consider Jack their friend. And like most little kids, Jack wants desperately to be big like them.

So when the lifeguard stopped us almost instantly upon our entry into the indoor water extravaganza, I could see Jack's heart rate begin to rise. "He looks too short," the lifeguard said to me, then snapped, "He must be measured." And he led us to the official measuring stick.

The closer we got, the smaller Jack looked. My heart ached for him.

The lady in charge of flotation devices took over so the lifeguard could go back to his monitoring duties. She motioned to Jack. "Stand here," she said, pointing to the measuring stick.

Determined to prove his manhood, Jack placed his back to the wall, took in a deep breath, and held it while standing as straight as possible. As he did, he seemed to grow.

"Hmm," she said. It was hard to tell if he was at or below the line.

With her brow furrowed, she leaned in for a closer look. Watching her inspect his height, Jack willed himself the slightest bit taller. Then she checked to be sure he was standing flat and gave him the best news of the day. "You're high enough." She nodded and gave him the go-ahead to move on.

Fury, his friend, and I breathed an enormous sigh of relief. And Jack zipped away from the measuring stick before the lady could change her mind. Off the boys went, walking—not running—and swam, slid, and lazy-rivered to their hearts' content.

As I experienced relief along with Jack, I remembered standing at the entrance of a roller coaster line with my sister and her friends when I was little, my plans to tag along thwarted by the amusement park's height-requirement sign. Those signs always looked so inviting with their smiles and cartoonish hands held up to show the necessary height. But they were relentless in their judgment. Often embarrassing. Sometimes defeating if one measured below the line, especially in front of people.

The failure to measure up can be devastating.

Measuring up meant the world to Jack as he stood next to a pile of life vests. While nothing in his person changed between the time he walked into King Spa & Sauna and the moment he stood next to *This High,* that measuring stick held his fragile esteem in its hand. If Jack made the mark, he was good to go. If not, the kid's worst fear about himself would have come true. He would not have been a big boy, but a baby in need of a life jacket. Even though his worth had nothing to do with *This High,* everything he thought about himself did. In that moment, a life jacket declared his status—for all to see.

I settled in on a lounge chair beside the pool and watched the boys. And I watched the other kids swimming alongside, laughing, playing, enjoying. I watched the parents. All shapes, colors, sizes, and ages congregated in *their* staycation fun. And I wondered about measuring sticks in their lives. What *This High* measurements hold their self-worth in the balance? A job title? A house size or location? A dress size? A school acceptance or rejection? A sports achievement? Inclusion in a social group? Inclusion of their *kid* in a social group? Is their peace and joy at risk the way Jack's was as he bravely stood and awaited the verdict?

Life's measuring sticks do more than set a mark. They introduce

You're Not Alone

I started a professional Facebook page not quite two years ago, thinking it would be a way to not only establish a network of connections but also to comfortably market myself (something I don't like doing, but which seems necessary in today's fast-paced, constantly channel-changing world). The goal of the page was to publish posts of relevant and interesting pieces from the world of psychology and beyond and intersperse affirmations and entertaining cartoons. I spend hours per day sorting through feeds and sites, not going to bed when I need to and putting off visiting with others, feeling pressure to post the best and most interesting pieces I can find. And while I have established a core group of readers, most of my posts go unnoticed (as measured by Likes). What I have discovered, however, is that in spite of what seems like a lot of work for little reward, people actually read the articles without commenting or liking. In fact, I was talking to a good friend today who shared he often reads my expectations. They present the perception of spotlights. They toy with our emotions and hold the power to make or break our dreams. We stand with our back to the stick and breathe in, hoping to grow an extra inch so we can measure up as we compare ourselves to *This High* in order to fit in or to be okay or to be Better Than, maybe even win. Whether or not we measure up in our comparison drives our

pieces and sends them to his daughter. He actually read one article and found himself changing how he spoke to his family that evening when he came home, measuring his words more carefully and thoughtfully.

All of the above to say that I no longer measure the worth of a post on how many Likes it gets. I post because it gives me pleasure and I know that somewhere, someone may be sending that post to his son, daughter, friend, or spouse.

For me, one of the biggest pitfalls of social media is the expectation and need for affirmation. Most of us in life will never go viral or be a Brené Brown, but we all make a difference in our own way. For me, it's the foul balls that count, not the home runs (those are few and far between, if ever). I have learned to trust that I do what I do because it gives me joy (and is a great way to keep up with current research), and anything more is icing on the cake.

—Amy S., PhD

contentment. The mark offers quite a bit of power to something that, more often than not, should have nothing to do with our self-worth.

I couldn't help but be convicted. Walking into King Spa & Sauna, I might have felt a tiny bit sorry for myself, dissatisfied that our water fun was taking place at an unknown indoor facility rather than beachside where "all" of my friends were. (Which of course isn't true. Comparison, more often than not, draws our focus to the few rather than to the many in our same situation.) Any other week of the year, I would have considered our Groupon adventure something like a badge of cool-mom honor. But since this was our vacation, my mind had flipped things a bit and tricked me to compare, concluding that somehow these memories would land in a Less Than category, not quite measuring up to the minimum. My contentment hinged on something that actually had no relevance.

And it certainly wasn't the first time in recent memory I'd measured life by the wrong yardstick.

MELTDOWN IN FROZEN FOODS

"Kay?"

Hearing the voice behind me, I turned to see the familiar face of a sweet woman I've known for many years. Though her kids are the same age as a few of mine, they attend different schools. Now, so unlike days past when our kids were little and we could meet at the park, we see each other only sporadically. This time we met up in the frozen-food aisle.

"How are you?" she asked with sincerity. "It's been so long."

"I'm good," I responded. "I'm so glad to see you. It *has* been a long time."

We exchanged a few pleasantries and caught up on the highlights of each other's lives. Then she asked, "How's Boxster?"

"You know," I began, "Boxster is doing okay."

"So is SB," she replied, before I could ask after her son.

And then she started to relate to me in rapid-fire mode SB's list of accomplishments. As you might guess, SB isn't his real name; it's the name I gave him in my mind, right there on the spot as I started to melt in the middle of the frozen-food aisle under the heat of all his teenage accomplishments.

Super Boy exceeds expectations faster than the speed of lightning and can leap any tall order in a single bound. He scored a 2400 on his SAT and plays first-chair cello while tutoring little children and quarterbacking the football team. He interns for his congressman and feeds starving children in the Sudan all from an app he created for his iPhone. Super Boy, master of everything.

"Have I told you about his Eagle Scout?" my friend asked. "He finished it faster than anyone in their troop. Ever. You know, he started later than other kids—sixth grade—and ended early. We couldn't believe it! Fastest in the history of his group." She paused as if to savor the words before continuing. "We're so proud of him. Not only that, he started high school a year ahead so is graduating early. And according to practice testing scores, he's on track for National Merit Scholarship Finalist. This summer, he's already got an internship working for

Company Z. They read the article in the newspaper about his scout-ing achievement and called *him*! Did you see the article? Front page of the Metro section?"

"We don't take the paper," I said.

"He made varsity lacrosse as a freshman, was voted onto student council. And in the strangest turn of events"—she paused to catch her breath—"we were stopped at NorthPark mall the other day by a scout-ing agent. Not for sports but modeling. We're headed to New York next week to see about that. I mean, have you ever?"

No, I have not. But my thought process had stalled somewhere back at her mention of the Eagle Scout thing, when my stomach tight-ened up with something close to panic. *We haven't done Boy Scouts,* my brain screamed at me. *You fool! How will Boxster get into any-thing without Eagle Scout on his résumé? Should we have pushed that? Push. What am I thinking? We never even introduced the idea. It seemed so time-consuming and inconsequential. Man, was I ever wrong! Can we turn back time? Start over? Have I ruined his chances?*

Rather than appreciating the truly remarkable things my friend's talented, and very nice, son had accomplished, I heard all the ways I've failed my child by not even introducing most of these concepts. As a family we tend to avoid a good many activities. Too many kids. Too much time in the car. We thought we were doing the right thing. But did we actually ruin his (all of their) chances at a successful life?

As I felt myself pulled down into an emotional sinkhole, I strug-gled to stuff my feelings of anxiety. *Just breathe,* I told myself, faintly hearing my friend's voice over my own thoughts.

Oh my word! Are the kids supposed to take practice tests for the PSATs? I thought they'd learn what they needed to learn in school. He hasn't done any practice testing. Neither has his sister. They aren't prepared at all! Are they going to fail? Can you fail the SAT? And an internship? And modeling? Seriously? We need help! Now!

Breathe, I reminded myself yet again. *How can I breathe? We're completely, life-alteringly behind the eightball. I knew it. There isn't "a college for everyone"!!!*

At this point, I'm 100 percent positive that I've blown it. I've done what I've dreaded since the moment a positive pregnancy test surprised me oh-so-many years ago. I've single-handedly ruined my kid's chances in life.

Mercifully, our conversation ended soon after that. We hugged and promised to get together soon. At least I think we did. It was all a blur at that point. I felt so sick, I worried I might throw up. Walking out of the grocery store, I was half the person who walked in, eaten up by anxiety and despair.

I felt Less Than.

Enormously so.

Measuring well below *This High.*

"What's wrong?" Snopes asked as we loaded our bags into the car.

I love that kid. Inasmuch as she calls me on possible speeding violations, points out every time I forget to signal, and corrects my misuse of words, she keeps it real. She could sense something was off. And she was right. I had just been gut-punched. Laid out for the count. In need of resuscitation.

What she didn't know, and what I had yet to realize, is that I had done it to myself.

"I ran into Mrs. B. when I was grabbing waffles. And . . . well . . . I just feel a bit sick after our conversation," I admitted as we climbed into the car.

"Why?"

"I don't know. She shared all the amazing stuff SB has been up to. But it was like I couldn't hear anything she was telling me. All I heard was how I was failing. She was sweet to share what SB was doing. But it made me feel like a complete failure."

A thought reinforced by the clutter from five school pickups and a pervasive aroma (we had yet to discover the culprit) in our car. I can't even keep a space as small as the inside of a car free from rot.

"Mom, have you forgotten those 'three little words'?" She playfully employed air quotes.

"What?" I was still reeling from the onslaught of negativity.

"Mom. The 'three words'?"

I couldn't believe she was tossing back at me our little conversation and the advice I had lobbed at her months earlier. Who's the adult here?

I realized that, just as she had the day the three words entered our world, I had let comparison reduce me to a puddle of Less Than. Right there in the frozen-food aisle, I had melted under the bright lights of another family's accomplishments.

The truth? SB is remarkable. He truly is. And on top of all that, he's a terrific guy. What's more, I love that friend. I honestly don't think she meant a thing by airing that exhaustive list of accomplishments. She was so excited for her son and rightfully assumed I would be too. The problem was in my perspective, how I made it all about me instead of declaring to my friend, "I'm so happy for you guys."

"You're right," I told Snopes. "I wish I had said those words, even if silently to myself. Honestly, I completely forgot. I don't know why. Maybe since I was caught off guard." It had been a long week, parenting-wise. "All I could think about was how I had missed the boat, ruined your brother's life by not doing Boy Scouts—"

You're Not Alone

When I was in elementary school and would come home either angry from being left out at recess or sadly alone at lunch, *and* when I would come home all *I'm the best* (weird that those could both be going on at the same place and same time), my mother told me, "Put your blinders on." I knew what that meant since we had horses. We had one horse in particular that would get so distracted by the others that if he didn't have his blinders on, he couldn't walk the trails.

Mom would tell me, "Don't look to the left or the right—and be careful turning around to look behind. You might bump into something while you're checking out all that should or could have been, and you just might miss out on exciting things ahead."

—Todd

"Boy Scouts?" she interrupted. "Boy Scouts did this to you?"

"Yes. Okay, so I know it sounds ridiculous. It's just . . . everything they're doing seems like what I should be doing. It's hard to hear and not wish it was me." It *was* ridiculous.

She just shot me a smile.

Later, my friend shot me a similar smile when our paths crossed again. I confessed my flood of thoughts and got to tell her how genuinely thrilled I was for them.

"Kay, I told you about all that because I know you love him." Then she went on to share, "It was so nice to get to walk through all that. To celebrate out loud with someone who cares. Truth is, that day we had gotten terrible news about another one of our kids. Bumping into you was so nice for me. It made me think about the good stuff instead of being consumed by the pending bad."

There's almost always more than meets the eye. I learned yet again that I need to get over myself and force my eyes to focus on the entire person rather than on the Glimpse I see in the moment.

Perpetual Motion

In so many areas of life, we beat ourselves with the yardstick of comparison, frustrated by all the ways we fail to measure up. And measure up to what? Who is it, exactly, drawing the *measure-up* line?

The bar tells me: *This is the level. If you reach it, then you're good to go. Everything will be great when you're This High.* But just as soon as we move into the "right" neighborhood, barely able to afford the tiny cottage, I can't help but be lured by the next thing. Apparently, we need to live on that other block in the great school district so our kids can attend the best grade school. But even in the right school, the kids need to be in TAG classes or on the advanced art or technology track.

And once a child makes the sports team, the pressure is on to join the club team. And then to climb the levels within the club to make the traveling team.

At work we need to land a job that makes use of that expensive degree. But the goal shifts the instant we secure that coveted job. Promotions, raises, title changes, team size. At one of my jobs, even the type of desk chair we sat in signified our level of importance. Each new level promises satisfaction and reveals a new mark we need to achieve.

We measure ourselves against other people who are measuring themselves against other people. Unlike the height requirement at King Spa & Sauna, there's no objective measure for how high is enough. We always need to stretch just a little more in hopes of reaching that ever-changing goal.

Measuring up is a tease. No one can call it a done deal. It reminds me of normal, another line that begs our attention. Being normal is okay. *Outstanding* is much better as it relates to normal. *Below average,* not so good. But like measuring up, normal is a relative concept.

I'll never forget sitting across the room from a medical professional who was meeting with one of our kids. I reeled as these words nonchalantly floated my way: "I said to your child, 'You're not normal. Let's work on that.'" His matter-of-fact manner, as if discovering a vitamin deficiency, stunned me.

Watching all my years of hard work—the careful laying of brick upon brick of self-confidence in a sturdy foundation the kid could build a life on—instantly crumple like a mobile home hit by a tornado, I wanted to yell, "You said what?!" But he kept going, and the kid seemed not at all fazed by the verdict.

Driving home with "not normal" sitting next to me, I searched for a spot to put this one. Isn't normal what we all strive to be? Isn't normal the goal? Isn't normal the only ticket to a happy life? I looked over at the kid and noticed he seemed a bit relieved, as if a ton of bricks had been lifted from his shoulders. I began to wonder, *Who came up with the idea of "normal"?*

Because, quite frankly, who is?

The next day I stopped by another child's classroom to drop off something for the teacher. As I scanned the room, I saw the learning disabled, the squirmers, the odd introverts, the attention-grabbing extroverts, the hotheads, the dreamers, the beautiful, the funny— basically, the mix. Normal must have been hiding somewhere in the sea of kids, but I couldn't see it.

According to Philip Zimbardo, Stanford Professor Emeritus and renowned expert in human behavior,

[Social] norms are the potential "pressure" in situations that: help to define the nature of social reality; form the foundation upon which people base their interaction; and provide a common referent for members' self-evaluation. By means of these mechanisms, norms increase feelings of personal and group identity.

Norms shape behavior by providing limits within which people receive social approval for their behavior. These guidelines establish an informal basis for estimating how far one may go before experiencing the normative power of ridicule, rejection, and loss of status among friends, acquaintances, and co-workers.[1]

There you have it: normal exists so we can fit in. And apparently we're the ones who decide what defines normal. We determine the height of the measuring sticks. We set the goal and move it. We keep it in perpetual motion.

> **Happiness is like a butterfly which, when pursued, is always beyond our grasp, but, if you will sit down quietly, may alight upon you.**
> —Nathaniel Hawthorne

Then we all strive to reach that elusive target. If we—or even better, our kids—are "above" the bar, we're pretty stoked and just might not be able to stop ourselves from sharing with anyone who will listen how special the "above average" can't help but be. If, on the other hand, we—or sadly, our kids—are "below" the bar, well, that's the worst of all spots. In that case, little is said and trainers or tutors are hired.

Wherever we may be, we constantly focus on how we measure up.

Therein lies the danger: self-absorption. Cue once again narcissism —being consumed by and with ourselves—stage left.

The truth is, we will never get rid of the measuring.

And some lines actually help. I'm glad there's a threshold of safety for my child as it relates to things like swimming at King Spa & Sauna.

I understand the necessity of measurements for academics, health issues, and the like. The problem isn't the existence of the lines but our relationship (sometimes obsession) with the lines. If I can interact with the measuring lines according to their intended purpose—in Jack's case, to assess safety—then great. But if I let the line define my self-worth, then I might need to do a little soul-searching. Any resulting dissatisfaction or prideful satisfaction with our placement on the measuring line can mess with contentment and happiness. Our obsession with measuring up to comparative indicators leaves us at the mercy of the law of perpetual motion, which continually readjusts the bar, holding us hostage to societal whims.

Instead, maybe our contentment and happiness should depend on something else. Shawn Achor, author of *The Happiness Advantage,* shares a provocative insight:

> Perhaps the most accurate term for happiness, then, is the one Aristotle used: *eudaimonia,* which translates not directly to "happiness" but to "human flourishing." This definition really resonates with me because it acknowledges that happiness is not all about yellow smiley faces and rainbows. *For me, happiness is the joy we feel striving after our potential.*[2]

This again points to a significant common theme in the search for contentment: "striving after *our* potential." Not someone else's, not a predetermined spot we measure ourselves against, but *our* unique potential.

Might focusing on the reality that we each have differing "bests" free us to spur others on to strive after *their* potential?

LINES OF SIGHT

Since there's no definitive mark for measuring up, it's utterly futile for me to try to reach it. In my parenting, in our household finances, in our vacation plans.

As is often the case, one of my children provided perspective.

"Mom," Snopes said to me on the last day of our staycation, "this was actually a great spring break."

Did she just say "great"? Even after all the grueling hours of aptitude testing? "Really, honey?" I asked in disbelief.

"Yes. In fact it was perfect. I wasn't so happy about the testing, but it did turn out great. And it gave me something productive to do. And I got to spend time with you. Real time. And I loved going to the movie together. Just you and me. And taking care of the boys, building forts with those huge boxes, jumping on the trampoline without having to be anywhere, riding our bikes, watching you and Jack build the puzzle over and over and over. It was so much fun. I'm glad we can have fun at home." She paused and thought for a moment, then added, "I really like that."

So we didn't go skiing. And we didn't go to the beach. But apparently we did make memories. Good memories. Because making memories can happen even at home. Contentment has nothing to do with *This High* as measured by comparison to others. And I learned that some of the most important destinations really can't be reached by plane or any other form of transportation.

Not all of our togetherness is pretty—cluttered car, sibling squabbles, and all—but even so I can't think of anything I'd rather do than be with my kids, especially now that the oldest ones are getting driver's licenses and can leave without me. (I'm going to be a humongous mess when the door opens to usher them to adulthood.) I'm all too aware that the years are slipping by. My hope is that home will be a sweet memory for each of them and that they will want to come back often. I hope it's a place where they know they're accepted and loved, regardless of how society says they measure up. A place where their worth is not determined by their ability to act or look a certain way but simply by their being who they were created to be. A place where they're challenged to reach their unique potential and to encourage and celebrate with others as they do the same.

Dare we hope the same for ourselves?

Letting Go of Comparison

Striving to reach an elusive This High, *as determined by societal comparison, leads to discord. Joy comes when we find harmony with ourselves and the life we're currently living, resting in our potential rather than being distracted by everyone else's.*

7

We Belong . . . Together

The Need to Be Known

> It is strange to be known so universally and
> yet to be so lonely.
>
> —Albert Einstein

*D*espite my inability to fully comprehend the wonders of technological advancement, I can't help but notice that, along with the good of timesaving and life-enhancing access to instant information, all these cutting-edge paraphernalia and apps pose numerous pitfalls. These traps point not to an inherent problem with technology but to the innate self-centeredness of human nature.

Most of us cannot imagine facing the day (or an hour) without access to a smartphone, which is in reality a handheld computer that puts the world at our fingertips. Daily, we navigate countless opportunities to "connect." At the core of how we respond to these opportunities lies one of the issues we've been considering: the need to belong and to be accepted.

I stop at a traffic light or sit in a carpool line or wait in a doctor's office and glance at my phone. Check e-mail. Maybe sneak a Facebook peek. Where I see my friend Bev sharing a fun pic of her beautiful family standing on the deck of their lovely Colorado home with a gorgeous mountain backdrop. Such fun. I wish I could be there. I mean, I actually wish I could be there. In my own Colorado home. Taking a picture of *my* family, sweetly loving each other, wearing complementary clothing, smiling angelically, and cooperating in a family pose, all draped in the beauty of the Rocky Mountains.

My brain swallows the bait:

We don't have a Colorado home.

We didn't even take a vacation this year.

We're completely missing out. Our kids are lacking. How will they answer questions like "Where did you go this summer?" or "What did you do over spring break?" or "Did you do anything?"

No.

How will I field the same questions when I run into friends at Starbucks? *And what are my friends doing together at Starbucks without me? Did they forget to call? And why are they wearing matching outfits? Oh yeah, probably because they play on a tennis team, together. At their club, where we don't belong.*

Which begs the question: Where do I belong?

Do I belong?

That's all any of us want. The need to belong is woven into the sinews of our souls. Simon Sinak, author and TED talker, sums it up:

"Our need to belong is not rational, but it is a constant that exists across all peoples in all cultures. . . . When we feel like we belong we feel connected and we feel safe. As humans we crave the feeling and we seek it out."[1]

That's what these kids are desperately seeking when they post and search for Likes. It's one reason Xbox and PlayStation lure kids of all ages into online gaming. In those communities they gain a sense of belonging and no one can be rejected based on outward appearance. A safe barrier of anonymity promises to keep the sting of judgment at bay as the players literally control their world. If things start to go downhill, they can simply power down or switch to another world where they can fit in or possibly even rule.

My biggest social nightmare in junior high was having a note passed *through* rather than *to* me. Today, a socially uncertain, incredibly sensitive tween or teen has the chance all day, throughout every day, to have his or her self-esteem secured or demolished on social media.

Kids gauge their social acceptance and standing by and through the Like or Share button countless times a day from the minute their heads leave the pillow—or round the clock, if they're among those keeping their phones under their pillow so they can be "connected" all night long.

I watched it play out in my car the other night while bringing some girls home from volleyball practice.

"Could you believe Sarah?" one gasped. "She jammed."

"Yeah, well, so did you."

"You too, girlfriend. Your serve smokes," added the third passenger.

"Really? You think so?" questioned my daughter, needing an extra dose of affirmation. "I don't know . . ."

"Oh, stop it. You know you're good. You're faking. No one can touch your serve when you get it over."

I really like that say-it-like-it-is kid. She called my daughter on the mat. Told her to accept a compliment. A hard thing for most of us to do.

"Hey, I like my hair right now." Another girl changed the subject. She must have flipped to camera mode and pointed it at herself.

"Selfie!" *Click.* "Here." She grabbed the girl next to her. "Get in with me." *Click.*

"Ohh. Let's do it like this." Head tilt. Pouty lips. The second girl holds up peace sign fingers. *Click.*

"Oh yeah. Tilt your head that way. I'll tilt mine like this." She angles her head and inspects. "Yeah, then my hair falls just right." *Click.*

All of this is going on at night. When the first flash lit up my entire car, I thought I was being pulled over by a policeman. For the next few minutes, I flashed down the road as they clicked, giggled, clicked, squealed, and clicked again.

Then the selfie-starter hit Send.

"Oh look! I've already got fifteen Likes. Awesome." She knuckle-bombs the girl next to her. "In less than a minute!"

"Let me see!" That's my daughter.

"Send it to me. I'll post it too," added the other friend.

The coolness gauge has been activated. They all look. They all measure. And they all care.

When I was their age, I cared too. I'd stand in the bathroom in the morning, curling iron in hand, doing my best to create wonders with my flat, unmotivated hair. I'd check out my skin. Worry about my bloodshot eyes. Contacts were relatively new on the scene and irritated my eyes, but they were an exciting step up from my wire-frame glasses.

I'd check out my clothes in the full-length mirror at the end of my room. The looking didn't help my confidence, but off I would go. From that point on, it was really out of sight, out of mind. Which is a luxury not available to today's kids, thanks to their phones. They can always be in the forefront of their minds or someone else's. They take selfies and post. Within seconds their self-esteem lies in the hands of

You're Not Alone

I have a friend that seems to have an amazing social life, always going to lunch with someone or on some exciting adventure. When I would see her Facebook posts, I would feel envious that my social calendar was not half as exciting. A couple of weeks ago, I went line dancing and she texted me she could go. I texted back that I was so glad she could make it. She thanked me and said it encouraged her because she was in a bad place with friends! It made me pause and reflect on the fact that we all have lonely, disappointing times in relationships!

—Helen

the thousand-plus "friends." Like an oarless boat riding the ocean, they rise and fall at the complete mercy of social-acceptance waves.

And somewhere in the striving for Likes and the accumulation of "friends," we find ourselves more alone than we were to begin with.

ALONE TOGETHER

Being alone in a crowd is nothing new. Think back to your junior high cafeteria. How can any crowd feel lonelier than that? The problem today is the trend toward isolation, especially from genuine human contact.

It's hard to believe that in an era offering arguably the greatest ability to connect with people, isolation is on the rise. Stephen Marche pondered the issue in an article in *The Atlantic:*

> We are living in an isolation that would have been unimagi-
> nable to our ancestors, and yet we have never been more
> accessible. Over the past three decades, technology has de-
> livered to us a world in which we need not be out of contact
> for a fraction of a moment. In 2010, at a cost of $300
> million, 800 miles of fiber-optic cable was laid between
> the Chicago Mercantile Exchange and the New York Stock
> Exchange to shave three milliseconds off trading times. Yet
> within this world of instant and absolute communication,
> unbounded by limits of time or space, we suffer from
> unprecedented alienation. We have never been more de-
> tached from one another, or lonelier. In a world consumed

by ever more novel modes of socializing, we have less and less actual society.[2]

With the arrival of the Internet of Things—connectedness via collected data from sensors and actuators in devices that we wear, carry, or own—we are pulling away rather than toward each other. Experts feel that interpersonal communication via actual human contact will continue to be pushed from the scene as "most of our devices will be communicating on our behalf . . . interacting with the physical and virtual worlds more than interacting with us."[3] Yet our inherent and basic need for relationship, interacting, and belonging will not change. We are hard-wired for *human* connectedness, connectedness that cannot be created by technology. With the societal trend toward everything-electronic comes some human interaction issues.

Sara H. Konrath of the University of Michigan at Ann Arbor recently led a study on empathy, which I think of as compassion with a little extra oomph. Empathy is the ability to feel alongside someone as he experiences happiness, grief, or pain. The results of Konrath's study offer cause for concern:

> Empathy is a cornerstone of human behavior and has long
> been considered innate. A forthcoming study, however,
> challenges this assumption by demonstrating that empathy
> levels have been declining over the past 30 years.

What's the culprit? Though the answer cannot be fully pinpointed, the experts have offered at least one theory: "Konrath cites the increase in social isolation, which has coincided with the drop in empathy."[4] Social isolation, in the midst of a crowd.

What so often gets lost in the social-media world is interpersonal relationships. Sure, it exists in the form of Comments or messaging. But not at all the same way it does in person.

Most of us don't have to travel far to witness the effects. The dinner table often says it all, especially at a restaurant. Add to the mix a grandparent who doesn't hold back frustration over devices that stifle conversation, and we see up close and personal the way we isolate in the midst of people.

Granted conversation at a mixed-generation dinner table has probably always been lacking:

"What did you do today at school?"

"Nothing."

"Really? Nothing?"

Silence.

But devices haven't helped. Even when sitting with their friends, even when husbands and wives or friends sit next to each other, the presence of technology more often than not inhibits human interaction.

I asked Andy Braner if he would share his thoughts about technology and connectedness on the *Moat Blog*. He comes at it from his perspective as president of a nonprofit teen outdoor center called KIVU. Here's what he wrote:

A major publishing house representative once asked me to name the number one issue for teenagers in the 21st century. She expected to hear *low self esteem,* or *teens face an education crisis,* or even something like *I'm sure if we could only keep kids from taking drugs we could turn this tide.* But without hesitation, I looked at her and said, "They're lonely."

"What? Lonely?" she said. "They're on their phones 24/7. They've got Facebook, Twitter, YouTube, and Skype. How in the world can any teen today be lonely?" . . .

[Kids] wander from their profile to their friend's profile.

They peruse the pictures their friend posted and think quietly, *Man, this life is awesome and must be fulfilling,* and all the while the friend is thinking the same thing and sneaking peeks of other walls—everyone searching for someone to find meaning with.

You see, we were created to be together. God made humankind and looked down at Adam and said, "It is not good for the man to be alone." When I read that passage of scripture the other day, I thought, *But wasn't God in the garden? Adam wasn't alone. What is God trying to say here?* And, I think He's trying to say, "I love you but I created you for community with humans."[5]

Granted Andy is looking at the issue of isolation with regard to teens, but are we not all just a flesh wound away from reverting to our junior high sensitivities? Our longing to fit in is exceeded only by our fear that we don't. We look around and compare, hoping to secure our place in this world by reading the right books, driving the right car, watching the right television shows. Our obsession with "right" is only exacerbated by our ability to see and know what everyone else is doing.

And we never feel we've done quite enough to arrive at "right" and to fully belong.

Is community with humans, as in interpersonal relationship and communication, the key to genuinely meeting our need to belong? According to Andy, yes. Practically speaking, yes. Even small, seemingly insignificant but deeply meaningful interaction fills voids.

WRAPPED IN A BURRITO

We go to Chipotle often. I think they put some addictive substance in their seasoning. Seriously, something drives my kids to think their day is not complete without a chicken burrito. Sort of how I view the iced tea at one of Dallas's finest, City Cafe To Go. If only I were joking. I hope my teeth can stave off the brown until I'm old enough to not care.

Anyway, although each franchise location offers the same menu, certain Chipotle locations surpass others, not because of what is served but because of *how* it is served.

"Mom!" Snopes exclaimed recently as she got into our car waiting outside the Preston Center location. Double-parked, I had told her I'd wait while she ran in and grabbed a treat for her and her brother. "Oh my word. He's just so nice."

"Who?"

"You know, CG"—as in Chipotle Guy—"who serves us."

She's right. He's crazy nice.

"When I walked in the door, he looked up from the register and smile-waved, like I'm some long-lost relative. Then he kept helping everyone else. I ordered our food, and when I stepped up to pay, he didn't even ask me what I got. He told me. He said, 'So you get the chicken, rice, and cheese. And your brother gets rice and chicken, with extra rice.' That's what he said." She paused to be sure I was listening, and continued, "Then he opened Boxster's to make sure they had put enough rice. He didn't think they had, so he took it back and added some with the hugest smile on his face, all while asking me questions about what I was up to."

Her story was making me smile.

"Then he said, 'Make sure you tell your brother that I missed seeing him today. It's been a while since he was in.' Then he went even further. He said, 'He's such a nice boy. You've got a great brother.' Oh my word. It was *so* nice. How can he be so nice? It's going to make Boxster feel so good. He made me feel so good."

"That's some rich stuff," I agreed. "But you know the thing about that story that will make Boxster feel the best?"

"Yes," Snopes replied after thinking for a minute. "That CG knew about the rice."

For sure.

"What do you think it is about the rice?" I asked.

She thought for a minute. I love that she thinks before she speaks. So unlike her mother. "I think it's that someone knows him."

She was right. "Being known. It's what we all want. Not in the famous sort of way, though I know you guys think that would be cool," I said. "But knowing us well enough to recognize the little bitty things that really mean something. Like extra rice in a burrito bowl."

"I want to be like him," she said, still glowing from the encounter.

"Me too," I agreed—and meant it. "I hope we all can be like that guy. Uplifting people along the way. Wouldn't that be fun?"

We both chewed on that thought as we drove home.

She knows all about the desire to be known. My word, as a teen, she's in the thick of it. She doesn't want to be lost in a crowd or to fade into the background. Same with her siblings. Same with me. It feels so nice to be known, whether by a Starbucks barista who starts making your coffee before you've reached the register or by the grocery-store bagger who greets you by name.

The seemingly insignificant act of not just filling an order but actually caring for the person put some major fuel in that girl's tank. And when we got home, it put some fuel in her brother's tank. While I entered the house and headed for the kitchen, she beelined upstairs. I didn't catch the beginning of their conversation, but I did hear them as they walked downstairs together.

"Can you believe how nice he is? I mean he even reached in the bag and took the lid off your bowl to make sure it was just the way you like it. You've got to see it."

"He really asked about me?"

"Yes! With that superfriendly smile he has. He's just *so* nice."

Crazy that extra rice could be so powerful. Clearly, knowing and being known—truly belonging together as humans—has nothing to do with Likes or Shares or trending.

I wonder who is walking beside me that needs some extra rice. I hope I'm looking. And noticing. I hope I'm training my kids to notice. Maybe then we can spread the happiness like our inspirational friend at Chipotle.

~~~ **Enough Already** ~~~

I deleted all of my social-media apps about two months ago for what was supposed to be a week-long fast, but I have yet to re-download those apps. And to tell you the truth I really don't miss them. I've realized I enjoy life more without them and ultimately I'm just more content.

An innate characteristic of social media that I hadn't previously thought about is the frequency of comparison. On Twitter and Instagram I yearn for confirmation that what I am doing and saying is "likeable." The way I satisfy this need is by getting more likes, favorites, and re-tweets. However, the worst part is that when I compare myself to other people on social media, I get jealous quickly. I am not the coolest, funniest, or most interesting person I know, and I have found that social media serves to remind me of that frequently. I live a great life, but sometimes I get so caught up in how great other people's lives look on social media that I forget about my own life.

That's why I'm no longer on social media, at least for the time being. While I think that those apps certainly have their upsides, and there isn't anything inherently wrong with them, they just aren't for me. Now, I am forced to have real interactions with people instead of just "following them." I get to find more productive ways of using my time. And ultimately, I am just happier . . . *Cue the song "Happy" by Pharrell Williams.*

—Jonny Wills

REJOICE WITH THOSE WHO REJOICE,
AND CRY WITH THOSE WHO CRY

The satisfaction that came from Snopes's encounter with CG offers proof that relationships—genuinely talking and communicating—have something to do with moving from comparison to contentment, predominantly due to the compassion aspect of such interaction. CG might not have labeled it compassion, but his interaction with Snopes was seasoned with it the minute she walked in the door. And the interaction warmed her soul and quite possibly his too.

Which is interesting to consider. We are groomed to believe that the best way to live is looking out for our own interest. But in reality, lasting satisfaction rarely accompanies that approach.

"I was going to be sad when Greer said she was going swimming," my friend Mandy's six-year-old daughter said to her as they left her friend's house. "But I wasn't sad," she explained, "because I knew I was going swimming at the Wymas."

Kids say it like it is.

Mandy tried to steer her daughter another direction. "Wouldn't you be happy for Greer to get to go swimming, whether or not you get to go, because she's your friend?"

Her daughter answered truthfully, "No. It's only fun if I get to go."

I laughed when Mandy told me about the conversation. That six-year-old little girl said out loud what we often feel, even though we try to cover it up with polite.

Mandy didn't let her daughter stop there because a life focused on our own desires is far from satisfying. Satisfying life is found in relationships and friendships where we can genuinely rejoice along with someone who is happy and cry when that person is sad.

And through those authentic and genuine relationships, we find that we belong, we are known, and we are accepted.

With its use of words like *Friend* and *Like,* social media lures us into believing that belonging and being accepted look like large numbers of both. But the truth is, depth wins out over width every time.

Mandy has been my friend for almost thirty years. Our friendship is tried and true, mostly because we are honest with each other. She's not afraid to call me out; she's a safe place for me to share; she rejoices when I rejoice and is sad when I am sad. And it goes both ways.

True friendship encourages and offers safe ground for authenticity, a rare commodity these days. Such friends don't judge, but they will tell you the truth even if it stings. They'll run your carpool at the last minute, listen and keep the info to themselves, come when called, cry or laugh with—not at—you.

> **Only your real friends will tell
> you when your face is dirty.**
> —Sicilian proverb

They don't leave you wondering whether or not you're okay. You don't have to prove yourself or strive to be anyone other than who you are, because with true friends you belong just as you are.

"If it's best to go it alone, God would never have put other people on the earth." I sound like a broken record as I yet again try to get this truth through to one of my kids who gravitates toward island living. And we're not talking Hawaiian or Cayman. He tends to isolate. Most likely due to past hurts, possibly due to insecurity, probably due to the fact that, given the sheer volume of people in our house, it's hard to find time alone.

Isolation leads us down the trail of self-absorption.

Friends—honest, loving, authentic friends—offer a path out. They come alongside and support us where and when we need it most.

I watched such a friendship play out in the pool the other day as I relished the genuine impromptu giggling of a few of the kids playing with their friends. I love such moments.

We have an inherited behemoth of a pool in our backyard. I think the hole was dug in the 1960s, at least two owners ago. It takes up most of the backyard. Which is actually nice for our size family. Upon taking ownership, we had to resurface the pool. And in the process we removed the old diving board and replaced it with a stone wall that now anchors that end of our pool. All of the kids love to jump and play games off it. Well, almost all. One has been eying it for months. Jack has ascended with trepidation on multiple occasions. Normally, he stands next to the older kids, looks below, descends, and opts to jump in the pool from the close-to-the-water sides instead.

But today he has decided to jump in from the four-foot wall at the end of the pool. Huge hurdle. I watched his little legs quiver as he resolved to follow everyone else's lead, scared of the deep end of our pool but determined.

He did it. He jumped. And since he's a little guy, he buoyed right back to the surface, lickety-split. As his head burst through the water, a smile spread from ear to ear. Crazy great.

But that wasn't all.

Apparently I'm living some weird Norman Rockwell day.

Rather than swim to the edge closest to the wall and get out, the kid began his slow, methodical dog paddle to the other end of the pool. Despite questionable technique, he can make his way the length of the pool. It just takes a while. A member of Dory's just-keep-swimming club, he kept his head above water and never for a moment considered stopping.

As I watched, I could see his fatigue. But he kept going. And here's where I just about busted with emotion.

A dark shadow grew under him. Was it the pool sweep coming close? a snarky middle-schooler coming to scare the daylights out of easy prey? What could it be?

The shadow was his sister, who had apparently been watching him too. She silently swam up underneath him and lifted him on her back. Another smile replaced his determined grimace as he lightly held on to her shoulders. They both happy-giggled as she moved back and forth like a dolphin carrying him to the other end of the pool.

What a beautiful picture of friendship. Because, in addition to being related to each other, they are friends. Genuine friends.

I loved what I saw.

And I wondered.

Who am I walking alongside in life that needs a lift? Just a thoughtful coming along beside or a boost of support? Because sometimes we need someone to carry our load for us. Sometimes we need someone to be honest with us. Sometimes, even when we're determined to make it on our own, we just need company.

And in being truly known, we truly belong.

Letting Go of Comparison

The measure of a life's impact is not about numbers or followers or reposts. Meaningful relationship is measured in authentic and honest accountability with people who aren't competing against us but who stand ready to ascend mountains and to travel the valleys with us.

8

Fair Play

Coming to Terms with the Inequalities of Life

> All some folks want is their fair share
> and yours.
>
> —Arnold H. Glasow

"Can I play with your phone?"

It's a question I hear a gazillion times. Daily.

"No," I knee-jerk reply. Apparently, he has not read the article about excessive screen time being number one on the list of the Ten Most Horrible ways a parent can wreck a child, especially between the ages of zero and six. And since he's six, I have only a few more months to make up for all the ruination I've caused by letting him play with my phone. The other four kids are already toast. I must make up for all my mistakes through him.

"Puh-lee-hee-hee-heeeezzz," Jack begs.

I can't stand begging. If the kids would only learn that a polite request almost always gets them what they want. But he just can't stop himself.

"Maaaahhhwwwm!" Only moms know how many bizarre ways that one syllable can be stretched.

"Not. Right. Now." My tone is firm, but my words have opened the door to possibility.

"But Fury gets to play," he moans. "Why does he get to play and I don't?"

"The answer is no."

His response is already a foregone conclusion. *"It's not fair!"*

Fury, sitting next to him and happily engrossed in his own game, says nothing. It's a kid tactic. Pretend like you don't exist by saying nothing. Then maybe Mom won't notice.

The injured party continues crying. "Why? He's playing. Why can't I have your phone?"

"First of all, I said no. And second, what you're doing has nothing to do with Fury. Seriously. Fury's business is not yours. What does he have to do with you?"

"It has *everything* to do with me." Full-on sobs have now engulfed his dramatic little self.

"Well, the answer is *no*," I zip. "And you just sit there and be quiet." So there.

Jack crosses his arms and musters a stonewall scowl accompanied by an audible *"Humph!"* followed by an extra *"Humph!!"* in case I didn't catch the first one.

My shotgun rider looks at me and shakes her head. "He sure gets mad."

"I know." After further consideration, it's hard not to admit, "I think we all do."

The kid sees what his brother has. He wants what his brother has. Then he claims the high ground of injustice. Because it's "not fair" for his brother to have or to do something he can't. Interestingly, if his brother had been sitting next to him with nothing, the kid would have been content with his phone-free state.

I've found myself detouring to the Land of Not Fair more often than I care to recall. I remember being passed over for promotion by someone who didn't deserve it as much as I did. He had a degree from a bigger school with a powerhouse MBA program. I knew that being able to flaunt that detail was worth a lot to my employer, but it didn't seem fair.

I also remember a high school tennis-team ladder that was decided on a match I lost because the weather affected my game. Spring tennis in West Texas wind is not for the weak. And since I'd held my spot for a month, I didn't think a single loss would determine our spots. But it did. One match in the wind lost my spot. Not fair.

I remember one of my kids being left out of a weekend trip with her best buddies solely because she goes to a different school. So she got to listen to them all plan the trip, and she got to sit next to them afterward and hear them whisper about the fun they had, because they didn't want to hurt her feelings by talking about it in front of her. So unfair.

I know, of course, that life's unfairness sometimes benefits me. I can only imagine the capable person unfairly slighted due to my company's desire to highlight before clients something from my employment history or education. I'm sure I've won a match and enjoyed a higher ranking due to someone else's bad day. And I know I've been privileged to be included in certain events merely because I was in the right place at the right time.

When I'm on the right side of fair, do I consider the ones who miss out?

Back in the car as we navigated the intersection of Injustice and Melodrama, my thoughtful shotgun companion offered one of her trademark insights. "It's funny," she started. "Not ha-ha funny, but, you know, funny like 'why does he make it so hard?'"

"Mmm-huh," I replied, careful not to tread over her insights with my own, for once.

"Well, he's making himself miserable. He could be so happy if he just let it be. You know? If he could just sit back there and be okay with Fury getting to play on the iPad, he would actually be happy. But it's like he would rather Fury have nothing and be miserable too than just be happy for him."

I managed to hold my tongue as she continued to process.

"Oh my word! I do the same thing," Snopes realized and admitted out loud. "I hate it when Barton gets to ride in the front. She races and beats me when I want it. And I make sure she knows I'm mad at her. Of course I deny it when she asks, 'Are you mad at me?' But I *am* mad. And I want her to be miserable and feel it, just to ruin her ride."

She smiled at me. I smiled back. "I can't believe you're admitting that," I told her. And I wondered if she was bummed she'd just confessed to something that I will more than likely point out next time it happens.

"I know I do it," she said. "And I know it ruins the ride for her—

and for me. It's terrible. I don't understand why I can't just be glad for her. It's like Jack. He'd rather you take Fury's game and make him miserable than let it be okay." She thought for a moment, then finished her assessment with a statement of fact. "I don't know why he doesn't try being happy for Fury. We all know you will give him your phone in a few minutes."

She was right. I did pass the phone back within minutes. So much for standing on principle.

When we arrived at home, Snopes got out of the car and opened the back to get our groceries. She divvied them out to the boys, and this time it was Fury who declared life unfair as he begrudgingly accepted his load.

"Why does Jack only have to carry one? I have *four*!"

Ahhh . . . the injustice of it all.

I made my way to the back of the car. "Stop it," I snapped. "Just carry them in. And if you keep complaining, you can carry them all."

"Boy, it never stops, does it?" Snopes asked.

"Probably not, honey." Then I added, grabbing a couple of sacks myself, "I think it's just part of the way we are."

Once inside the house, Barton helped me put away the groceries, and the boys raced for the couch, hoping to find respite from my cruel and unreasonable requests for their help. Engrossed in whatever game had captured their attention in the car, I heard Fury scold the brother who was now playing with my phone, "Quit with the yay!"

Apparently, Jack was happily exclaiming "yay" every time he did something good on the game. Since they were playing the same game, every "yay" was an arrow piercing Fury's soul with envy.

"Did you actually say 'Quit with the yay'?" I asked.

"Yes," the kid sheepishly responded. "I don't like hearing him win."

"Oh. My. Word." I couldn't believe the grip resentment could have on these boys. "What does his winning have to do with *your* game? You're not even playing against each other!"

"I don't want him to win," said super-sensitive-I-need-a-nap kid.

Okay, so he probably just said what we might sometime think deep down.

Fair Warning

What is it about fair that gets our goat and makes us jump on the oh-no-you-didn't train?

The other morning indignation over a presumed-to-be-unfair situation sent one member of our household over the edge. Since it was Saturday, he assumed, based on recent history, that donuts would be part of the breakfast equation. When offered a waffle, he fell apart, citing a litany of reasons why he should have donuts. The dramatic protest ended with his pointing at the table behind him and wailing, "*They* got donuts!"

"We're eating cereal," said his brother.

"What?" Donut Boy asked.

"Yeah," added a sister. "Cereal."

"Oh. I guess I will have a waffle, then."

All that righteous anger faded away when he realized others were suffering the same dismal fate. One of the biggest problems with trying to make life fair is that fairness is a shifting scale, usually based on what everyone else has. Which leads to the rather obvious insight that it is impossible to define something as fair or not fair without contrasting and comparing. Like preschoolers at a party, instead of being grateful for the cupcake we have, we're looking to see who got more sprinkles on theirs.

> **Lower your expectations of earth.**
> **This isn't heaven, so don't expect it to be.**
> —Max Lucado

Children proclaim what's "not fair" out loud and with conviction. While most adults have learned to temper responses with a bit more sophistication and less gusto, at least in the open, we are almost as quick to assert our claims of fairness similarly based on *entitlement* or *injustice*.

Entitlement: I Deserve It!

Apparently we feel entitled to certain things, as if life itself or our parents or other people owe us something. These entitlements might include a car at sixteen, a clothing allowance, designer glasses, a promotion, a window office, a covered parking space, or three weeks of vacation. One of our children thinks we owe him a college education.

"You're paying for my college," he commented to me one day.

"Why would you say that?"

"Well, because that's what you're supposed to do. I'm your kid, aren't I?"

"Yes."

"So you pay for my college."

I tried to explain to him. "That's not a given. I'm not sure where you came up with that, but your dad and I aren't necessarily walking that road. Do you understand that Dad's parents didn't pay for *his* college?"

"Well, that's different."

"I'm not sure how." I always wonder how much of anything I say to the kids sinks in; teenage ears seem particularly resistant. But I still try. "You need to be mentally prepared to cover it yourself. You can't think you're owed because you want it or because your friends have it or whatever."

In our home, I've found that many declarations of *unfair* arise from an assumed progression gone awry. It goes something like this, "Boxster got a phone in fifth grade. When do I get mine?" The injured party often calls on comparison to underscore her claims: "*Everyone* has a phone. And not some flip phone, but a smartphone. *I'm the only one* who doesn't have one. And now that I'm eleven, I get one, right?"

The same selling points are highlighted in conversations about viewing movies:

"Mom, there's this movie that everyone *loves*. It's so good. I really want to see it. Can I go?"

"What is it?"

"*The Best Movie Ever.*" (Doesn't really matter the title, this is how my deprived child will think of it.)

"Honey, I'm going to need to check it out." (I try to remain open-minded, but experience has shown me that if it's PG-13 it's likely to be overly violent, racy, peppered with foul language, or all of the above—not ideal material for a newly minted teen.)

"What?! I'm *thirteen*! Do you not trust me? Seriously?! Everyone else gets to go. I can't believe this!"

Mmm-hmm. I'm in the midst of Round Three with the "I'm *thirteen*, Mom" argument. I've got two more to go after this one.

PG-13 wears me out. Rating people, moviemaking people, do you have children?

I can't blame my kids for wanting to see the latest, greatest film all their friends are talking about. But as my husband and I emerge from yet another mortifying movie experience endured for the purpose of vetting its suitability, I know my answer to the eager child will be, "I'm sorry. You can't see it. I wish I hadn't either." I will yet again be considered the prude and an unfair "mean mom."

You're Not Alone

My kids for sure live comparison out loud in "not fair." One came home yesterday complaining because her brother got a treat. Her *unfair* came in the form of small bites—not some overwhelming revelation, just constant annoyance keeping her from contentment. I watched her mind race as she pelted me, "I had two days of testing and I didn't get anything. Then I hurt my toe and you didn't let me get a Slurpee! *And* you never brought me flowers at my cheer competition."

—Ann S.

And once again my child will turn to the "it's not fair" argument in a fruitless effort to change my mind.

"Not fair" shines a bright light on all that is wrong in a world that doesn't go as we expect or think we deserve, especially as we compare our lives to what others get to have or do. For my child today it's a movie. I've ruined her life. Embarrassed her forever. But deep down, I know she knows that I love her enough to stay the course, though she's so mad she can barely stand to look at me.

Tomorrow it will be "the best party in the world. Everyone's going!"

"Will there be alcohol? Are parents going to be there?" In the race to be included and cool, underage drinking abounds despite being illegal.

"I can't believe you would ask that! Oh my word! Do you not trust me?"

The bigger question, the one that will determine if my kids can look beyond "I deserve" and "I expect" and stop wallowing in the unfairness of it all, is the one I could ask of them: "Do *you* trust *me*?"

When I pour salt into the wounds of injustice and respond to my kids' cries of "But whyyyyyyy?" with "Because I said so," I often tell them, "Whether you like it or not, I actually am the authority over you. You may not always know why I choose to give or not give you things you desire, and sometimes my decisions seem unfair (especially when a sibling seems to receive different treatment), but you can rest in the fact that I love you and have your best interest at heart. And I see a little more of the big picture than you can at this stage."

Of course that falls completely flat. They look at me incredulously and loudly wail yet again.

"It's not fair . . ."

I hear it all the time.

Often in my own head. Because I can entertain *unfair* thoughts too.

Financial author and radio host Dave Ramsey, after reflecting on the habits of wealthy people and being grateful for his own good fortune, offers important perspective:

> The talents and treasures on this earth are not distributed
> equally, and that is not fair—or is it? God has chosen to
> give most of you better hair than me, to make Tiger Woods
> a better golfer than me, to make Brad Paisley a better
> guitarist than me, and to make Max Lucado a better writer
> than me. With God's grace, I am fine with that. I am not
> angry at them, and I don't think they have done something
> wrong by becoming successful. As I've matured, I've come
> to realize that God is indeed fair, but fair does not mean
> equal.[1]

I do think our hang-up with what's fair and what's not leads back to a question of trust. Do my kids trust me? Do I trust the authority over me? Do I really believe God has my best interests at heart, even when someone else seems to have a better life? Do I trust that God is fair—and let *fair* not mean *equal*? Can I rest in the certainty that, in the end, justice prevails? I can if I completely trust the authority over me to execute that justice.

Injustice: I Don't Deserve This!

At the core of many, if not most, of our concerns with fairness lies the question of justice. And if justice is involved, I want to know, is the judge good? trustworthy? safe? My answer to those questions will shape my reaction when life doesn't go my way.

If I look closely enough at what propels comparison, I discover that fear is a major driving force. Fear that I might be forgotten or left out or left behind. My obsession grows when those I love might be the ones "robbed" of what I deem necessary for their best lives.

But those fears melt away if I can trust the judge to be fair, to ultimately desire what's best for all involved. Obviously, that doesn't mean life itself will be fair. I have several very dear friends battling cancer. Their young children watch day in and day out, not really sure why Mom's hair is gone or why she's in bed or why people keep bringing food to their house. Nothing is fair about those situations in this moment.

I have a friend whose industry is downsizing. Over the past ten years, she's held five different jobs, as one company after another got bought out and downsized by a foreign entity. Since she's in human resources, it fell upon her to basically fire everyone as those in charge closed their Texas shops. Then, the icing on the cake, she got to fire herself. To say her road hasn't been easy is an understatement. But she's navigated each detour, and the very long months of unemployment in between, thanks to one thing: faith. Though far from easy, what could she do but trust that everything would be okay because God is in control.

There are countless examples, but one very "not fair" is a story I've been reading about David and his friend Jonathan, son of the powerful King Saul and heir apparent. But God had other plans. And in knowing the throne would go to his friend David, Jonathan was happy. His joy wasn't sapped by the seeming unfairness. He even celebrated the one who would be king.

> And Saul's son Jonathan went to David at Horesh and helped
> him find strength in God. "Don't be afraid," he said. "My
> father Saul will not lay a hand on you. You will be king over
> Israel, and I will be second to you. Even my father Saul knows
> this."[2]

He even went so far as to encourage David in his own struggles. How could he do that?

I think it had something to do with placing his trust in God rather than in his circumstances.

Such trust allowed Jonathan to care for and encourage those around him rather than be consumed by *fair*. He wasn't obsessed with getting ahead or fighting for his fair share, which as the son of the king would include a crown of his own. Instead, he found contentment in accepting, embracing, and doing his best with the reality of his situation.

I need to remember that. Remind me that in the midst of financial issues, health challenges, imperfect relationships, broken appliances, and frustrated hopes, I can choose to be grateful and to trust that God has everything in hand and my best interests at heart.

But trust can be a challenge.

CROSSING STREAMS

Every Thanksgiving we gather with all my side of the family at my parents' home just outside Cave Creek, Arizona. I love Arizona and its low-key nods to nostalgia. The names of the streets tell it all. Have you been looking for Easy Street? It's just outside Scottsdale, next to Ho Hum Road and Tranquil Trail. Stagecoach Pass and Bloody Basin Road run parallel to Long Rifle, with Sidewinder doing what it does best, twist and turn.

Sometimes at night, I imagine what it must have been like in the days before electricity. The desert night, even with landscape lighting, bathes the world in a deep darkness that settles into every crevice, the stars so close they dare you to reach out and touch them.

Last year, we decided to pack up a couple of cars and take a day trip to Sedona. Before having kids, we did the same thing, taking a memorable hike through Oak Creek Canyon, soaking in all the red-rock beauty. Fueled by those memories, we made the trek in order to relive our glory days and let the kids roam.

When we arrived at the mouth of the canyon, everyone bolted out of the cars, younger ones running ahead to explore and discover. The kids had a blast finding the trail, getting lost off the trail, traipsing through the creek, yelling by the canyon walls and hearing the echoes, playing tag, and laughing with each other as they made memories.

Apparently, though, our own memories had been clouded by nostalgia or sleep deprivation. Somehow we had forgotten that Oak Creek Canyon's trail crosses its creek at least seven times. Not a problem. Unless two of the kids in your crew are visually impaired.

Never be afraid to trust
an unknown future to a known God.
—Corrie ten Boom

These two kids never cease to amaze us. They live life to the full. Never once have they considered their impairment to be a disability. The teen boy has even accompanied his brothers and cousins to summer camp. *Regular* summer sports camp. He's just like everyone else, so why not skateboard? Why not jump off the "Screamer" high dive?

"I'm the only cousin that jumped," he informed us one year. "No one else would do it." I suspect they might have chickened out once they looked down.

Visual impairment does have its advantages. And disadvantages. "I love playing dodge ball," he told us. "I just don't understand why I'm always the first to get out." Uh-huh, go for the blind kid. Actually, most of the campers never knew he couldn't see. He doesn't let on that he's blind, not as a game, but mostly because he never allows that minor fact to define him. He's amazing that way. As he was on that hike.

When we got to the first crossing, my heart sank. But that guy couldn't have cared less. He jumped right across without so much as a thought about the prospect of getting soaked.

His sister, however, was a bit less eager to get wet. Especially since it was cold outside. And the moss-covered rocks, though a welcome bridge, are slippery when wet. As a sighted person, I find them a bit challenging to navigate. Snopes and I walked up behind her, not sure what to do.

Without a word, my brother swept in beside his daughter. She wanted to cross. He was there to make sure she did.

"Okay, Mags"—his gentle voice found his eighteen-year-old daughter's ear—"put your hand right here on my shoulder."

Which she did. Without so much as a hint of hesitation.

"When I say 'right,' step forward with your right foot. Do the same thing with your left. Don't let go of my shoulder," he told her. Then he added, "I'll get you to the other side."

She smiled and put her hand on her father's shoulder as he directed. And they were off. "Right." "Left." "Forward." "Okay, this one's a little slippery. One hundred degrees left and grab a little tighter." "Now forty-five degrees right." Jump, hop, smile, laughter. They were on the other side.

Snopes and I, waiting our turn, looked at each other in disbelief. How did they do that? We were terrified to follow after them. Not sure we could do the same even if we'd been holding David's shoulder.

Maggie was racing up the next trail before we finished spluttering our way across the stream. I tried to be graceful. Really to no avail. Another nephew, waiting patiently behind me, shook his head in slight disgust.

"It was horrible, wasn't it?" I said, describing my graceless crossing of the stream.

"If only I could un-see it," he matter-of-factly replied.

146

"And to think your Uncle Jon married me after we hiked through this canyon together in our single days," I laughed nervously, hoping to regain some composure by poking fun at myself.

No such luck.

"That's a lot of love," he replied, as he passed me and headed up the trail after his sister.

Walking behind our crew, my mind lingered on the beauty of our creek crossing. That young lady, facing uncertainty, didn't waver for one second as her hand gripped the shoulder of her father. Was it fair that the other kids could see better or run faster along uneven surfaces or (fill in the blank)? Interestingly enough, *fair* never entered the conversation.

The daughter and her father displayed trust in action. She never tensed her muscles in fear, she never pulled back in uncertainty. She wasn't angry that everyone could race ahead. She listened to his voice—a voice she knows well—followed his instructions, and safely crossed.

She trusted him.

Completely.

I couldn't help seeing the lesson that played out right in front of me. *Complete, action-based trust* in someone whose intentions center on love. She did trust and she made it across in what could only be described as a crisis. For her to step on one of those rocks in the wrong way, or miss altogether, promised, at best, a cold, wet, miserable hike. Broken appendages, a cracked head, or worse were perhaps more likely. But she didn't face the trial alone. Her father walked beside and watched the trail ahead.

What a reminder of the heavenly Father who walks beside us and fully knows the way ahead, who is ready and willing to cross with us our streams of crisis and disappointment that so often seem unfair.

Maggie could trust her dad to get her across the stream because she knows him—intimately. In the same way, the degree to which we know our heavenly Father determines the degree of our trust. Such trust conquers fear and quenches concerns about what's fair.

Letting Go of Comparison

Fairness is a shifting scale, based on our assessment, accurate or not, of what others have. Contentment is found in accepting, embracing, and doing our best with the reality of our own situation.

9

The Side to Side

Our Obsession with Others

Persons appear to us according to the light
we throw upon them from our own minds.

—Laura Ingalls Wilder

I'll do it!" I eagerly volunteered at Fury's municipal swim meet. At
the beginning of the summer, I had signed our fourth child onto a
neighborhood swim team. I'm sure I thought about the meets at some
point between filling out the application and writing a check. But I
must have forgotten where we live and that "outdoor" is the operative
word for swim meets. Outdoor and limited shade. Going to a summer
swim meet on a blazing hot Texas afternoon is like willingly sitting in
a convection oven set on Broil.

So when the meet organizers asked for volunteers to write ribbons,
I was quick to raise my hand. "Yes," I confirmed. "I can do that."

So what if I had never written ribbons. How hard could it be?

"Where should I go?" I asked. Okay, so I knew where to go. I just didn't want everyone to know that I knew and that I was racing for the shade. The only shade. Shade with ceiling fans. Ceiling fans and coolers filled with ice-cold beverages, free for a ribbon-writing volunteer's taking. And people. New people. People with whom I could sit and chat in the shade, away from the relentless rays of the hot Texas sun.

Upon gathering my things and joining the ribbon-writing crowd, I quickly realized why no one else had volunteered. It was a mad dash to insanity from the minute I sat down until well past the end of the meet. There would be no drink grabbing or pleasant chatting. The other ribbon-writing parents and I frantically gathered times and other heat information, sorted, added, averaged, sorted again, and wrote ribbon after ribbon after ribbon in a valiant effort to do what our world has deemed right and good: reward every single participant multiple times over with accolades, warranted or not. But that's another story.[1]

My hand ached; my head spun. I tried to explain to the gal sitting next to me, "You know, my kids won't even let me help them with math homework. Numbers and I have issues." She didn't really listen. She was too busy trying to stay ahead of the speedy conveyor belt loaded with race results. But she smiled, a pained smile, the kind Ethel smiled at Lucy as they stuffed chocolates in their mouths and clothes.

"Hey!" a lady across the table shouted to me. "Isn't that your kid's heat?"

I was touched that she'd heard the announcement and knew that my boy was about to race. When I'd first sat down, a couple of parents realized that this was my first go at the ribbon-writing rodeo. They advised me to get the heats from my boy and write them on my arm in the same way they were written on his arm. Then when the heat number was called, I could take a quick break and watch him swim. It was neat how our little group banded together, trying to write and listen at the same time so we wouldn't miss our own children swimming.

"Oh my goodness." I nodded at her. "You're right. Thank you!"

So I put a couple of pens on my stack of events, marked my spot, and raced from my seat to the side of the pool. After searching the lanes, I found Fury, head bobbing in and out of the water, swimming the breaststroke.

The breaststroke is not Fury's forte. As crazy as it is, the kid's favorite stroke is butterfly. Pure agony for us regular folk. In fact, you couldn't pay me to swim butterfly. But in all the ribbon-writing frenzy, I had missed his butterfly, and I was grateful to get to watch him swim something.

I'm not new to competitive swimming. Swim team was a rite of passage for the kids in my family growing up. My dad made all of us competitively swim for at least two years. He was determined that we would feel at home in the water. I didn't like it then, but I'm grateful today for the swim-team experience. So much so that we've followed my dad's lead by requiring the same for each of our kids.

Memories of my own swim meets flooded my mind as I watched Fury breaststroke his way down the length of that pool.

Too bad I didn't stop at memories.

While watching Fury swim his heart out in lane four, I somehow started to channel the traits of my swim-team coach. Visions of Theron H. Pickle, coach of the Wichita Falls Mighty Ducks, filled my mind. Boy, could he yell. It never mattered how far away or deep underwater one might be, you could hear Coach Pickle cheering out a rhythm to follow. "Hup! Hup! Hup! Go, go, go!" Watching from the edge of the pool as Fury pulled through the water, it came back to me like it was yesterday.

Apparently, I remembered out loud.

Every time Fury's head came out of the water, I yelled, *"Hup! Hup! Hup! Go, go, go!"* getting louder and louder the farther he progressed.

You're Not Alone

As our children grow up, we think the parental competition will end. At last the kids have all been potty trained, given up pacifiers, and learned to read. But no, in our "I've got to be a little better than you" society, it continues. Issues change from whose baby slept through the night first to who scored the most soccer goals and escalates for the high school–aged child to who made cheerleader and National Merit scholar, who got what SAT scores and what Ivy League university they were accepted to. As if this isn't enough, can't we please graduate from this comparison game when our kids graduate high school? This road has been exhausting. Surely it is over.

But these achievements are quickly followed by sorority and fraternity pledging, summer internship jobs, and studying abroad. Okay, I breathe a sigh of relief that I have made it through all of that *and* my child has graduated *and* has a

Failing to realize I was the only one yelling (who knew that coaches—*and parents*—don't bark at their swimmers anymore?!). I frantically, at the top of my lungs, added to my "Hups" and "Gos," "Quit looking! . . . *Don't look!* . . . Go! *Hup, hup, hup* . . . STOP LOOKING!" Because every time the kid's head came up for air, he was checking out the lanes next to him. It was ridiculous.

Lost in the moment, I didn't grasp the intensity of my yelling until

real-life full-time job supporting himself. Can I please breathe now? No, of course not!

Wedding bells are ringing, and there is no better way to show your true love for your child than to throw the biggest and best celebration of the joining of these two tender hearts. It is a true gift from God for them to find the spouse who you have prayed for throughout the whole life of your child. So step number one, the ring!—Oh, and how many karats is that? Now, the joyous plans begin. As decisions are made, questions filter in from acquaintances about reception location, sit-down dinner or buffet, number of wedding attendants, size and type of flower arrangements, brand of bridesmaid dresses, the latest and greatest wedding photographers, and hopefully far-off exotic honeymoon plans.

Is it over yet? My friends with grandchildren say never.

—Elizabeth

I glanced over at the timers perched at the end of his lane and saw them looking at me in bewilderment. One of our friends, who happened to be standing behind the timers, bent down and reassured them, "That's his mother." I watched them shake their heads, feeling sorry for Fury, and I quickly zipped my yelling.

My kids are right. I *am* embarrassing.

Fury, accustomed to my weirdness, did nothing but shoot me a little smile-shrug when he got out of the pool. Then he walked over, and I gave him a big hug, proud that he'd tried so hard. In fact he won his heat.

"You did great," I said.

"Really? I think I won."

"Maybe. Good stuff." We started to walk back to his team's staging area. His looking around still on my mind, I added, "You know, you might have won your heat, but I'm not sure about the event. It's not a big deal one way or the other, as long as you did your best. But you might have been a bit waylaid by looking around to see what everyone else was doing."

He looked at me sheepishly. He knew and I knew (basically everyone positioned by the pool knew) that almost every time his head came out of the water, not only was he overwhelmed by my "Hup-ing" but was slowed down by his neighbor-checking.

"Your race really isn't against those kids swimming next to you," I continued. "It's against the wall. Swimming races are made up of heats. Your heat could be fast or slow. There's no way of knowing. So in reality, you're not racing against the kids who happen to be in the pool at the same time you are. You're racing for the wall."

He appeared to be listening, so I kept going. As if I could ever stop myself. "You need to focus on the wall. The wall is where your race ends."

In the water, Fury had gotten lost in the moment. He didn't realize that his side-to-side checks were distractions that slowed him down, even got him off track. He didn't understand that his obsession with what everyone else was doing affected, possibly determined, his outcome.

FINGERS POINTING BACK AT ME

The poolside lesson that day was simple and inconsequential in the grand scheme of things. Encouraging Fury to race to the wall might help him the next time he dives off the starting block, but even if not, he'll continue to relish the challenge of a good race.

Whatever my son took away from our conversation, I certainly learned a lesson from him. As I pointed out the effect of his focused-on-others approach, I noted the three fingers pointing back at me and realized the overwhelming inferences for my own life.

Looking from side to side, comparing myself to others, tracking my performance in reference to fellow sojourners has significantly more power than I realize. In a best-case scenario, comparison distracts. The looking from side to side, the obsession with others, slows me down.

But continually measuring my progress against others often has an even more detrimental impact. It takes my eyes off my own goal and my unique purpose, and it leads me to believe I need to keep up or get ahead or change to fit in. Worse, comparison can take me completely off course. It lures me into someone else's lane, fools me into thinking their path is better than mine. Caught up with moving into lane after lane in hopes of finding the right/fast/best one, I may never actually reach the wall.

And worst of all, although side-to-side glances place my focus on what others have or are doing, they actually plant my thoughts firmly on myself. Whether the measure is positive (I'm ahead) or negative (I'm behind), comparison guarantees self-absorption and discontent.

WHAT ABOUT THE OTHERS?

Comparison centers on the others who represent or remind me of all I should have, do, or be in order to live my best possible life. In laymen's terms, it's called envy. Through conversation and consideration, I've concluded that the others against whom we tend to obsessively compare ourselves fall into three distinct categories.

The Far, Far Aways

"I'm not sure all comparison is bad," my friend Cynthia told me. "Don't get me wrong. I can make myself sick as I compare in certain areas of life. But sometimes comparison inspires me." This accomplished interior designer and shop owner went on to describe her world. "I look at the people that do what I do as featured in *Architectural Digest* or certain magazines—huge projects from some of the world's most accomplished designers—and I learn from them."

These people, the untouchable types, are what I consider the Far,

Far Aways. They tend to be famous. We know their names, but we don't know them personally. We admire, possibly aspire, from afar.

She continued, "I look at what they've done, taking note in case I want to apply some of their techniques or glean from their expertise."

I think we all do something along those lines. When I was on semester in France, I could barely walk through any of the major art museums in Paris without seeing a student parked in front of one of the masters, copying and learning from colors and brush strokes. In

---

~~~ Enough Already ~~~

Coveting material goods in ads isn't the big hurdle for me. My real weakness is jealousy of others. The relentless comparison to my peers. Am I more successful than Julie's ex-boyfriend who invented a lighting gadget that fits over the page of a book so you can read it at night? It's been featured on the cover of the Levenger catalog, as my mother-in-law reminds me often.

If it's not the ex-boyfriend, it's someone else. And this type of coveting will never be assuaged. If by some crazy quirk or twist of fate or accounting error, I were to get J. S. Foer's speaking fee, then I'd move right on to coveting Madeleine Albright's speaking fee. The Bible is right. Jealousy is a useless, time-wasting emotion that's eating me alive. I should focus on my family and, nowadays, God.

Of course, stopping an emotion is not easy.[2]

—A. J. Jacobs, *The Year of Living Biblically*

---

the same way, we can learn from the masters in our own fields, gleaning while trying to keep our unique approach. There's no jealousy in that. I think Cynthia is right: not all comparison is bad. In certain situations it has the potential to inspire.

When I worked in Washington, I had no problem admiring from a distance people like the Chief of Staff or the Special Assistants to the President. Sure, my friends and I dreamed of one day rising to their pay grade, published for all to see. We were in awe of those folks who seemed to have attained such a pinnacle compared to our low-level life stage. But they prompted inspiration, not jealousy.

It's the same in all areas of life. As a mother, I have no problem openly celebrating the efforts of women far outside my social circle, from historical times, or maybe even speakers from a stage. I can easily, genuinely be happy for the Far, Far Aways.

The Alongsides

When people get closer to my turf, comparison produces a little less happiness, a little more tension. I tend to take closer note of those whose path I share, even though we're not walking together through life on a daily basis.

As a writer, I don't personally know too many of the authors in my genre, but I can't help but wonder about their success. As in, I wonder why them and why not me? What do they have that I don't? My recent blog touched on the same topic, so why did theirs get a hundred thousand Shares and mine got two? But I can stop myself easily with a reminder that the other person has been doing this longer and so naturally has a larger audience.

When someone whose orbit is just a bit larger than mine gets the accolades, I can be reasonably happy for him or her. But when the action moves slightly closer to home, my stomach hurts. It clenches with jealous tension as I note her prominent article in the *Dallas Morning News*. I desperately want to be thrilled for her success, but a green haze clouds my vision and makes me choke just a little. I really am happy for her. But *sort of* looms in the background with *not really* close behind.

In a sermon on jealousy, William Brownson, former professor of preaching at Western Theological Seminary and radio host, admitted to sharing this struggle with being happy for someone against whom we might feel ourselves competing. He noted that "the more important the activity was to me, the greater the problem I seemed to have." In high school sports, for example, though he might have outwardly been cheering for the whole team, inwardly he wasn't, especially if one classmate in particular was chosen over him to play in the game. He would offer the obligatory congratulations to his teammate (rival) on a game well played, even though on the inside it made him literally feel a bit sick.

Maybe you chuckle at that. That's just an immature, childish trait, you say. Maybe so. But I find it hard to shake even in my later years. When my sons took part in team sports, I felt at times the same pressures working on me. Let's say it's the day of the big game and some other lad is playing ahead of my son. Somehow I can't be as glad as I should when that young man excels. I am envious. I seem to want that position, that opportunity, that honor for my son. And most coaches know what a problem such fathers can be![3]

It's hard to be genuinely happy for Alongsides.

The Wish-It-Were-Me Achievers

We all have people in our lives who seem to always land on top, people whose successes compel us to stare and compare and crave. We just don't get it. Why does everything seem easy for them? Here's where we face a brutal struggle with the ugliness of envy and the less-than-productive thoughts that come with coveting.

I can deal with the success of other writers, because much as I'd like my work to rise to the top, that's not my main concern these days. But when I'm hit with good things happening to other people's kids, that's a bit more challenging. Why was his child chosen over mine as an honor council rep? Did you not see how honest and upstanding my daughter is? I mean, really. Honor council has her name all over it. And so does student council and the varsity volleyball team and so much more. Because my child should not be sitting on the bench. Right?

Again, I want to be happy and excited for the other family. But truth be told, I sometimes wish it were me. Worse, dare we admit that we might feel just a tinge of glee when a crack appears in someone's got-it-all-together veneer? It's terrible, but true.

I was talking with my brother-in-law, a psychiatrist, about how we sometimes find an odd sense of happiness in the misfortune of others. Jon and I have talked about it before. He sees it in the workplace. I see it in the parenting world. Haven't we all seen it at one time or another? Let's say the star quarterback, who also starts on the lacrosse A-team and was elected student body president, gets a slight injury—nothing life threatening—that benches him for a couple of games. In some strange way, mixed emotions play with the minds of parents whose kids didn't make the starting team or win the popular vote. And there's a little "Yeah, he needed to taste what the rest of us experience" mentality.

"I find it so interesting," I told my brother-in-law. "It amazes me that something slightly sinister sneaks into the psyche, even when no one means to have any ill feelings. Because you really do feel bad for the kid—and yet a little happy at the same time. It's a bit sick."

You're Not Alone

I noticed myself almost being happy—well, maybe not happy but finding some weird satisfaction—when my friend (I can't believe I'm admitting this, or that I even thought it) failed our board certification test. I've often caught myself looking at her. She's cute, has a nice boyfriend, lives in a great apartment, has the latest phone, and just bought a new MacBook Air. I'm sure not hurting for anything, but still, when I passed the exam on my first try and she failed, I found some sense of solace. I'm not proud of it.

—Rosalyn

My brother-in-law nodded in recognition of a familiar problem. "There's an old Russian proverb that I tell my kids, and patients, that applies to our innate nature associated with such reactions," he said. Then he proceeded to relate it:

In the days when the czars ruled Russia, there were a very few wealthy landowners and hordes of impoverished serfs. The serfs tilled the landowners' fields to eke out a living.

Two such serfs, Ivan and Boris, plowed fields that were next to each other, and they were allowed to keep a fraction of the harvest to feed their families. Ivan had the good fortune of owning an ox, which he could use to plow his field. Boris, even poorer than Ivan, had to put the harness over his neck in order to plow his own field.

Every day as Boris pulled his plow, he looked over at Ivan plowing with his ox, and his envy grew.

Then one day Boris's fortunes turned. As he was plowing he heard the clink of metal against metal. He ran back and saw that his plow had unearthed a metal box. With excitement, he pried the lid open and out popped a genie!

The genie said, "Boris, this is the day of your dreams. I will grant you one wish but, whatever it is, choose carefully."

Boris looked across to the neighboring field, where Ivan was walking freely behind his ox and plow. Boris thought long and hard and said to the genie, "My one and greatest wish is that Ivan's ox would die!"

My brother-in-law continued, "I heard this from another doctor, who I'm sure passed it on from someone else. It is the dilemma of all human beings as we think that joy will come from what we own. But in the struggle against our lower nature, we often feel 'good' fortune when someone else is experiencing misfortune. Maybe it is the Russian equivalent of the German term *schadenfreude*. I read that the literal English translation of that word is 'Harm-Joy.'"

If we can be transparent enough to admit such a struggle, maybe we can get rid of those weeds of envy that can grow deep when unattended. I'm sure that away from the situation, even poor Boris could see the futility of such a selfish approach. Maybe he needed a friend to snap him back to reality and open his eyes to the fact that they both could have an ox. Life would have been so much better if he could have peeled his eyes from comparison.

My friend Robin Pou pointed out to me the other day "Sure, comparison robs us of joy. But it steals more than that."

He continued, "When we are focused on wanting what someone else has, we've right there, in that moment, substituted our unique giftedness for theirs. When I compare my kid to the superstar whatever, I'm saying that God made a mistake by making my kid a certain way because he's missing what the other kid has. And in the process, his identity and purpose get lost. So not only are we tearing down our kids in the midst of comparing what they do or don't have to those around them, we're actually stealing their unique identity and purpose."

I thought about that the other night at dinner.

While waiting for our food, the kids began to doodle.

I sipped my tea and I watched and I noticed each child doing his or her thing. Always up for a game, Jack was playing tick-tack-toe with anyone willing to join in. Next to him one brother had drawn a wild scribbly something. A sister dreamily created a seascape filled with dolphins and starfish, anchored by a bright shining sun. Then a brother who can't turn it off had filled every blank space in front of him with equations building off each other, flanked by geometric shapes to match. Still another sister played creatively with very different geometric shapes, using them to form abstract letters.

> ## Everyone is gifted—but some people never open their packages!
> —Wolfgang Riebe

A future graphic designer? scientist? marine biologist? mechanic? I don't know; they're all so different.

And I started to breathe freely.

And I asked myself, *Am I loving them well?* Really loving them for who they are, not who I want them to be or think they ought to be or who society says they should be? Am I loving them for the special individuals they are? Am I helping them discover their unique gifting and building them up in that? Even when such gifting might take them down a road that looks a bit different from what I or everyone around me expects or values?

Each child is uniquely gifted. As are the adults at our table—and the surrounding tables. So why do we let envy get our goat and steal our attention?

Racing Alongside, Not Against

Most days, I'm not even aware that my thoughts are being held hostage to comparison. It's become almost instinctive to measure goals, accomplishments, and events against what someone else has achieved or gained.

Certainly healthy comparison can inspire us to reach higher and farther. There's nothing wrong with a young athlete admiring an Olympic champion and aspiring to one day reach a similar status. And an entry-level employee should be humble enough to believe she can learn from those farther along on their career path. But when our preoccupation with what others around us are thinking or doing begins to dictate our own thoughts and actions, we're entering dangerous territory. In our constant measuring, our assessing the size of the gap yawning between *them* and *us,* we unknowingly become obsessed with self. Our thoughts turn from healthy inspiration toward jealousy, insecurity, fear, justification, judgment.

Francis Schaeffer, an American theologian, philosopher, and Presbyterian minister, said so much as he contemplated covetousness:

We should love men enough not to envy, and this is not only envy for money; it is for everything. It can, for instance, be envy of his spiritual gifts. There is a simple test for this. Natural desires have become coveting against a fellow creature, one of our kind, a fellow man, when we have a mentality that would give us secret satisfaction at his misfortune. If a man has something, and he loses it, do we have an inward

pleasure? A secret satisfaction at his loss? Do not speak too
quickly and say it is never so, because you will make yourself
a liar. . . . If this mentality is upon me, in any way, then my
natural desires have become coveting. I am inwardly coveting
and I am not loving men as I should.[4]

So here's the surprising thing about the side-to-side glance: it
doesn't have to steal our joy.

What if, instead of looking at others as a measure of our own
value, we looked at them simply to appreciate and even celebrate their
successes? What if, instead of racing against them, we viewed ourselves
as racing alongside them, each of us reaching for our own personal
best?

William Brownson so beautifully points us to one of the biggest
problems with envy:

It shows a lack of appreciation for my own uniqueness and
worth. When you and I envy another person, we aren't even
seeing ourselves. The other one, the envied one, becomes
all-important to us. His gifts, her successes, their achievements!
We spend our energies watching someone else, being threat-
ened by that person, not wanting him or her to succeed. So, in
the process, we don't develop our own potential. . . .

Suppose we can see the successes, the accomplishments,
the victories of others as [God's] gifts also. That puts them in a
different light. . . . When I'm doing that, I discovered, it's hard
to keep on envying them. I find myself beginning to celebrate,

to rejoice in, what God is doing through them. And that's a victory I could never win by myself. It's a gift of grace.[5]

Maybe looking at others as we travel through life is inevitable, but what we take away from it doesn't have to be. Am I racing to the wall, embracing the challenge? Or am I frantically comparing myself along the way, viewing others as competitors whose position defines my worth?

The thing I'm beginning to realize about Obsessive Comparison Disorder is that it has compelled us to adopt for ourselves goals that were never ours to begin with. Goal setting is important when they're *our* goals. They help with direction and keep us going when we're tired.

Goal setters know that the mix should include some easy achievements as well as some that require us to stretch. Several years back, I started a cookie-mix company with a friend. We set achievable sales goals, then I threw in a pie-in-the-sky target. "Let's create a product that will sell in Neiman Marcus," I told my friend. I figured such a lofty aspiration would compel us to come up with a quality product in classy packaging. Believe it or not, it worked. But if our goals had been too small, we never would have made it as far. And if our goals had been driven by someone else's—a direct competitor, a larger company, a business standard—we would have been rubber-necking our way to paralysis.

Whatever the goal—a successful product, academic aptitude, athletic accomplishment, a healthier body—the race is to the wall, spurred on but not defined by others' performances.

If I can keep in mind that the wall to which I am racing has been uniquely predestined and calibrated to my specifications, I can break free from envy and discontent. I can be happy for you when you hit a home run. I can find satisfaction in doing *my* best.

Letting Go of Comparison

Life's race is to the wall, spurred on but not defined by others' performances. The only worthwhile goals are those based on our own individual giftedness.

Best Practices

Beware of the Superlative

> To be nobody-but-yourself—in a world which
> is doing its best, night and day, to make you
> everybody else—means to fight the hardest
> battle which any human being can fight; and
> never stop fighting.
>
> —e. e. cummings

With beautiful weather upon us, park time has reentered our picture. Blessed to live less than a block away from one of the prettiest parks in our area, we often grab tennis rackets or soccer balls or volleyballs, then race to see who gets there first. "We" might be a bit of a stretch. On most days, I plop my lazy self on a bench and watch Jack, my only one still willing to use the playground, maneuver his way around the park's cool equipment.

I enjoy few things more than watching kids play—running,

pretending, chasing, and laughing—all with a little intermittent whining for good measure. Amid the free-flow fun, a dichotomy is almost always in play at our park. On one recent visit I observed that instead of a couple of kids hitting the tennis ball, laughing and learning the game together, the courts were filled with personal coaches tossing balls to aspiring athletes under the watchful eyes of their hopeful parents. A few feet away, another trainer towered above a young man, barking commands sure to guarantee standout sporting prowess. From jumping jacks to running with a medicine ball to quick footwork drills, the budding athlete went through the motions, then raced to a car where a parent had been watching and waiting. And around the corner, a personal soccer coach talked one young star-to-be through his paces while another waited patiently for her turn. Two parents stood on the sidelines, politely chatting while sizing each other, and their children, up.

> **Excellence is not being the best,**
> **but doing your best.**
> —Author Unknown

While taking it all in, I struck up a conversation with the stranger next to me, one of my many habits that drive my children crazy. The other mom and I quickly discovered that her son and my youngest are close to the same age. She started to explain how they just didn't know where to put their boy for kindergarten. He had done so well on entrance exams (kindergarten entrance exams!) that they just couldn't decide. The pressure of nurturing his academic acumen was complicated by his athletic ability. "It's hard to make decisions with so many options these days," she told me, as if I could commiserate.

I looked at poor Jack, who had never played an organized sport. He sure can color though and deliver mail. That's his favorite activity at the moment. Drawing pictures, then delivering them to all the neighbors. Jeff, the eleven-year-old next door, could fill a few trash cans with all the "letters" Jack has colored for him.

So there I sat in a park filled with aspiring contenders for "Best in Show." So many around me seemed to be striving for the superlatives: hiring trainers, coaches, and tutors to help their child be the smartest or fastest or strongest, to ensure a spot on the winning team, to guarantee acceptance to Ivy, to . . . the list seems to go on.

And really, can anyone blame us? Because that's what we're supposed to do, right? Strive for superior? Be the best?

I was still mulling that park visit when I later read an article titled "Educated and Jobless: What's Next for Millennials?" from National Public Radio. The journalist interviewed Barry Schwartz, a psychologist at Swarthmore College, to discuss the seemingly endless options for this generation, but it was his ideas about "best" that caught my eye. Schwartz described how well-intentioned parents instill high expectations in their kids, who then feel like failures when an achievement is good, maybe great, but not perfect.

What Schwartz says he tries to tell his students is that a good job is good enough; they don't need to have the best job.

"If they can go through their lives looking for and appreciating what's good in their friendships, in their romantic relationships and in their work—even if their work is more modest than it would have been 10 years ago—they can live an incredibly satisfying life that way," he says.[1]

Which leads to the question: Is implying/insisting that we, or our children, need to be *the best* a good thing? Or does it set us up for chronic dissatisfaction as we watch others grab top posts and wonder when it will be our turn? Does it leave us unable to settle fully and happily into good jobs, good relationships, and good homes furnished with good appliances rather than the best? I mean, why commit yourself to something good when best might be just around the corner?

But does the best even exist?

MEASURING BEST

I'm convinced that *best,* like *normal,* does not hold a specific place on life's measuring stick. Though we stand on the shoulders of *-er* (better, smarter, faster) to position ourselves closer to best, we can never quite reach the elusive superlative. As soon as someone hits the mark, another striving soul jockeys for best and the line shifts again.

I grew up in a glass-half-full family where we threw words like *best* around without giving them deep thought.

"How can both your dad and your brother David be Charles's best man?" Jon asked when my younger brother was getting married.

"What do you mean? They're both best," I matter-of-factly replied.

"Well," he said, trying to gently explain the obvious, "*best* means 'better than everything else.' There's nothing better than best. There can only be one."

"Well," I stammered, wondering why he wouldn't want to live in our superlative world where lots of things are best. (It's my mother's fault. She's very positive.) "I guess he's using the word to mean a Best Dad and Best Brother so . . . together they are Best Man?"

Yeah . . . my explanation didn't make much sense to me either.

But when it comes to life, we can get caught in the current of need-to-be-bests. From schools to teams to coaches to party invites to jobs to marriage and even to church, we all seem to be striving to find or to have or to be the best. Yes, bizarre as it sounds, there seems to be a fascination with attending the best church, as if that exists. The thought is almost oxymoronic. How could one church or ministry set itself ahead of another? Yet we hear famous names or attendance numbers floated our way from the stage to confirm that we are in the "best" company as we worship.

Whether in ministry or elsewhere, the numbers game drives our world. We live in a strange culture that leans toward quantifying. How many attendees, subscribers, viewers, Likes, fans? How does your son's GPA compute? How many goals did your daughter score? How many steps did you walk today? And as we compare our counts with those of others in and beyond our circle, we either bask in the warmth of being Greater Than or feel a bit sickened by our Less Than status.

Because standout status is the key to satisfaction—or so we seem to think.

In the 1990s business strategist and author Tom Peters coined the phrase "The Brand Called You" in a *Fast Company* magazine cover article. The cover's tagline declared, "You Can't Move Up If You Don't Stand Out." The blurb explained, "Big companies understand the importance of brands. Today, in the age of the individual, you have to be your own brand. Here's what it takes to be the CEO of Me Inc."[2]

Peters later tweeted, "Remember: Excellent 'Brand You' portfolio about self-LESS-ness, not self-ISH-ness. You are as good as network you develop-nurture. PERIOD."[3] However, like many things that started with good intentions, the personal branding movement has taken on a life of its own, one where relationships are used to strengthen our brand. Making a name for ourselves has joined forces with age-old business strategies to create a whole new segment of marketing: Brand Me. Unfortunately, that shiny exterior hides a gaping pit of aloneness and stress and discontent that mark "the age of the individual."

Personal branding demands that we clearly and distinctively define ourselves. Who am I? I need to be able to present myself in a sound bite or at the very least in a short phrase (140 characters or less). Our personal brand needs to have a consistent message across all platforms: blog, Twitter, Pinterest, Instagram, Facebook, LinkedIn. And if we're doing it right, our followers will share our brilliance on their blogs, Twitter feeds, and Pinterest, Instagram, Facebook, and LinkedIn accounts.

Branding is also underscored by what we do. And if doing one thing is good, juggling several is better. Now that we know more about what's going on in everyone's world, we feel a newfound pressure to do and to be the impossible—everything to everyone at the same time: funny, compassionate, environmentally sensitive, culturally aware, physically dynamic.

The United Kingdom's *Guardian* recently published marketing strategist Dorie Clark's tips to build Brand You in the year ahead, which include the following suggestion:

Sharpen your narrative: What do you say when someone asks: "what have you been up to lately?" Don't waste the opportunity, as so many do, with a ridiculous platitude ("not much" or "same old, same old"). It's important to make sure you always have something to contribute to the conversation, which shows you're staying current and interested in new challenges. Talk about a charity you've been volunteering for, or the most exciting project you're doing at work.[4]

Should we point out that in sharpening a narrative, we've taken over a conversation, an opportunity for relationship, and transformed it into a marketing opportunity? Forget about the person on the other side of the dialogue. And "Talk about a charity you've been volunteering for"? That strategy instantly undermines any charitable others-centeredness and makes what could have started as compassion just another measure for comparison, as we add volunteering to our striving-for list.

The narcissism of making a name for ourselves is palpable. C. S. Lewis describes the vice as only he can:

Now what you want to get clear is that Pride is *essentially* competitive—is competitive by its very nature—while the other vices are competitive only, so to speak, by accident. Pride gets no pleasure out of having something, only out of having more of it than the next man. We say that people are proud of being rich, or clever, or good-looking, but they are not. They are proud of being richer, or cleverer, or better-looking than others. If everyone else became equally rich, or clever, or good-looking there would be nothing to be proud about. It is the comparison that makes you proud: the pleasure of being above the rest.[5]

As we consider all the many ways to make Brand Me *best*, magazines and websites shower us with helpful hints, often numbered for our convenience. It's so much easier to fix something if there are "10 Easy Steps."

- "7 Things Smart Learners Do Differently"
- "8 Ways of Thinking to Make You Become Rich"
- "31 Questions That Will Change Your Life"
- "30 Vital Things Your Future Self Will Thank You For"
- "20 Excellent Websites That Help Children Learn Smarter"

If these don't fit, Lifehack.org has many, many more ideas for how you can improve yourself. New ones every day. It would be terrible to go a day without improvement. Or to commit one of "The 10 Biggest Blunders That Keep You Away from Success."[6]

Lists are made and shared as if they hold the answer we are all looking for: an instruction manual on how to be okay. But more often than not, the questions and lists confirm our fears that we are not measuring up to expectations—ours or anyone else's. The sheer volume of opportunities to improve ourselves, to make Brand Me better, overwhelm us and make it almost impossible to live—just live—life.

In an interview with Bryan Elliott, Seth Godin—author, entrepreneur, and marketing guru—pointed out, "What human beings do is art, is new stuff, is connection, and this humanity is what has been

You're Not Alone

I'll never forget listening to a CD in my husband's car. I grabbed his keys to run an errand and was forever moved by what I heard that day. He had been listening to a sermon titled "Heaven, a World of Love" by Jonathan Edwards. The words I heard were like an arrow to my heart. I struggle so with living up to expectations and I can't stop myself from comparing. What he said gave me perspective that I had never considered, an eternal worldview on comparison.

In an almost mind-numbing heady way, Edwards reveals that in heaven we won't look on anyone with envy or pride. When we look at people flourishing in their efforts, it won't be comparing ourselves to them, but basking in the beauty of God's work *through* them. We will be happy for them, not want to be them or look for some way to be better than them or be happy that I am better than them . . . but be happy *for* them. Like really.

And if it's that way in heaven, why not try to see God's working through people now rather than be jealous or feel inferior? It's pretty heady, but stopped me in my tracks.

—Leslie B.

boiled out of us." He then referenced the culture-changing "The Brand Called You" article and commented, "My new thing is, I am not a brand. You are not a brand. You're a person. And there's a big difference between being Dell and being Michael Dell. And I think that we're now entering this world where it's okay to be a person again."

Brands push an idea of the best, as if it exists. And maybe in products it does. But when we're considering people, *best* doesn't exist. Somewhere along the way, in our aspirations to be the best, we seem to have lost sight of the person—both ourselves and others. Godin went on to say, "It's all about how you can connect with people, how you can bring them up. I think there's not enough of that in the world."[7]

THE FRAGILITY OF FACADES

In our determination to be the best Brand Me we can be, some of us build facades, presenting to the outside world not our real selves but the one we desire to be. I'm reminded of the story about the Tower of Babel. At a time when "the whole world had one language and a common speech," a group decided to set themselves apart from the rest. They desired to be different and to be noticed.

> Then they said, "Come, let us build ourselves a city, with a
> tower that reaches to the heavens, so that we may make a name
> for ourselves; otherwise we will be scattered over the face of the
> whole earth."[8]

If they didn't make a name for themselves, they would be scattered, indistinguishable, regular in the midst of all the other people. Which absolutely wouldn't cut it. Not then. And not now.

We, too, bake bricks, then we put them together into monuments to our own importance. The bricks we bake and use may differ based on our environments, the families in which we grew up, our talents, even our insecurities. But for most of us, the bricks we stack up include the following:

Our home. The location, size, amenities, drive-up appeal, and interior decorating all communicate a lot about who we are and what we value.

Education, ours and our children's. In certain circles, names of top schools drop like rain into conversations as indicators of a person's status or presumed intelligence. If you live in New York City, get ready; it starts young.

"A consultant got my daughter into uptown Montessori," one mom said. We . . . mothers were huddled in the indoor playground, frantically discussing—what else—our preschool attempts. "It's a Dalton-feeder."

"Nice," another nodded over the mini-trampoline. "It's all about exmissions." . . .

The opposite of "admissions," "exmissions" is the process of getting students out of the school. Many parents were madly concerned about which kindergartens the preschools could get them into. (Message boards exist where parents analyze the preschools' "TT"—top tier—hit rate.)[9]

In Dallas we may not be quite that intent on educational pedigrees, but names are dropped and heads nod in admiration (possibly jealousy) or shoulders relax in silent relief as LT (low tier) school names are shared and the competitive bar is lowered.

In Starbucks the other day, I couldn't help but overhear the discussion between two elderly men ahead of me in line. Really, I think everyone heard—and I suspect that was the intent. They were Rolodexing their latest endeavors, mostly boards on which they served and businesses in which they were or are involved. It was so interesting to listen to the name-drop Ping-Pong game. And with almost every name came a well-known alma mater. I guess the poor folks whose names that stood alone must have attended a non-pedigree school.

Activities. Athletic? Musical? Techy? CrossFit? Whatever the case, activity choice—and the relevant wardrobe selections—informs onlookers' assumptions about who we are. I have a friend who owned a popular sandwich shop in our neighborhood. She would chuckle at all the ladies dressed in their cute tennis outfits coming to grab lunch to go. On occasion, she would ask how the game went. "You wouldn't believe how many told me they don't play," she said. "Once, one confessed she wanted people to think she was on a team. I guess simply wearing the clothes makes us feel better about ourselves."

Wardrobe. Labels, formerly relegated to inside the waistband or inside-collar of clothing, now adorn the outside for all to see and admire—or snub. My Sam's Club, Costco, and Stein Mart winners aren't always appreciated for the great buys that they are by those more fashionably minded than myself. Especially by my teenage daughters. (They'll learn.)

Friends. It's who you know, baby—and how casually you can drop their names into a conversation.

Driving a recent carpool, I couldn't help but sigh as one of the young riders in my backseat honed those name-dropping skills. I don't know if the kid meant to or not, but whenever he used the name of one friend whose family is well known, he consistently emphasized the last name.

When I lived in Washington, DC, people had "power walls" where they displayed photos taken with the most elite of Who's Who. How many they had and which faces were featured said a lot about a person's status. Whether or not the pic was signed said even more. And was it personalized in Sharpie? An autopen signature is for posers.

These days, selfies with celebrities dot social-media walls. " 'I love the adulation and the number of "likes" that my friends post,' Parihar, twenty-four, says. He also saves all his prized selfies."[10]

Christmas card letters. We love them; we hate them. Sometimes it's hard to read all the great stuff going on in someone else's life without wondering what in the world is wrong with us. My friend Lana sent a different version a few years ago. Here's a brief excerpt:

> Dear friends, neighbors, relatives and probation officers, . . .
>
> Tip is looking good but is so busy with work/travel, Boys Scouts, volunteering at the Arboretum, church, building a tree house, Indian guides, financial planning, sailing, home repairs, children's sporting events, and mountain climbing. He gave up sleeping about a year ago and is now considering giving up work. . . .

Also, to set the record straight, since inquiring minds want to know; our children have **not** scored the most goals on their soccer teams (they mostly play goalie), are **not** the top student in their grade level for all of north Texas (but they are doing well and can spell *succotash*), are **not** all Eagle Scouts (Elizabeth is a girl you know), have **not** won the Nobel Peace Prize (although they would be a contender if they could make peace in this house). . . . They are great kids who are fun and make our life rich in love and joy!

Now you can believe whatever you want of our biography above (although most of it is true).

Love, the Housewrights

Kids. Dare we admit that we look to our kids and grandkids to determine our worth? Lana with tongue in cheek touched on that painful truth in her Christmas letter. As we allow, maybe even use, our kids to determine our worth, we lose sight of our own unique abilities and quite possibly stifle our kids' unique offerings.

Other bricks can include a title at work, our outward appearance, full calendars, volunteer efforts, awards, and so many other aspects of life. Brick baking and facade fashioning have become the driving force in much of our decision making. *How will this play on the résumé? What about a college application? Who might take notice when I post this on Facebook?* is so much a part of life that we go about the work business as usual. We look at the facades around us to determine what ours should look like. And we search for just the right mortar to hold it all together.

But how often do we simply follow our inclinations and interests without worrying about trends or what others might think?

Funny thing about those towers we're building: they're extremely fragile.

> **True humility is not thinking less of yourself; it is thinking of yourself less.**
> —C. S. Lewis, *Mere Christianity*

Jack loves Legos. He has an eye for and fascination with symmetry, so he quietly works for hours searching for just the right pieces to build his own vehicles, buildings, landscapes, and figures. Recently I watched as he carefully crafted three different, perfectly symmetrical "robots." He stood them up on the table where he'd been building and rested his head on his hands to admire the creations. He didn't call attention to anything. He simply found pleasure in what he built.

I then watched as an unaware brother raced through the house, aiming to get to the trampoline before his sister. He lost his footing and, as if in slow motion, slid into the table where Jack's robots stood. Let's just say, the robots didn't have stable bases. They wobbled, tipped, and tilted on the table before sliding off and crashing to the floor.

The towers we build are as fragile as those Lego robots and just as easily fall to pieces. Unexpected events come along. A jarring bump from unmet expectations or unfair occurrences or even from the consequences of a bad decision can abruptly send our efforts crashing.

And we stand, like Jack, staring at a pile of bricks.

Except, unlike Jack and his Legos, the crash doesn't simply break our creations; it exposes what's behind the bricks. Scrambling after the dislodged bricks, we race to put it all back together before someone sees the real person behind the facade. The effort to keep it all together so we look a certain way is exhausting. And futile. And actually not necessary. The struggle to maintain appearances is yet another way comparison chains us to performance and leads us away from contentment.

Not What I Do, but Who I Am

Last year, Barton tried out for the volleyball team at her school. She was a tiny bit nervous since most of the other girls play on club teams. But she made the team anyway and loved it.

Not playing on club teams is a family decision. Barton's older sister played on a club team for one season. But no one in our home liked how it ruled our life. Having to be somewhere on a regular basis cramped our laid-back, do-nothing style. After mentally multiplying that times five, we concluded it's not worth it—for us.

To help Barton further develop her skills and confidence for this year's season, I offered her a couple of camps, some clinics, and practice with her sister's school team before tryouts, but she said no to all of it. She loves the game and figured she would step up and do what she did before. Well, she stepped up, but apparently it *wasn't* enough. At the end of a stressful tryout week, we looked on the coach's web page. Her number was missing from the team roster.

My stomach hurt. My heart ached for her as she stared at the list in disbelief. Sadness took over. (At least it took over me.)

We refreshed the page a couple of times in hopes that maybe it was a mistake. Could I have clicked on the seventh-grade team instead of eighth grade? Was that 47 actually a 41, her number? I hadn't. It wasn't. She didn't make the team.

Within moments, I had to leave to take her brother to his middle school cross-country meet. I hugged Barton and told her how proud I am of her and how much I love her. Then I got in the car and gave myself a mental beating as I combed through all of the "should haves" and "would haves." We should have done the club route, then she would have made the team. I should have forced the camps and clinics, then she would have gotten what she wanted. I should have been a better parent, then she would have been included and have a group to fit into. I blew it. Our life approach has, in fact, ruined hers.

Then I forced myself to stop.

Failure and disappointment come with the territory. Beyond, even in the midst of, the heartache lie some absolutely golden life lessons. Because one day she will undoubtedly be passed over for a promotion; she will most likely fail to get into a college she wanted; she will be left off a party invitation list; she won't be picked; she won't be chosen . . . The list goes on.

What a great opportunity to walk this road next to her, not for her.

Little did I know, she was already—though begrudgingly and with a little disbelief—starting to navigate this detour on her own. She bravely responded to the excited "Did you make it?!" texts from friends and now former teammates. And their responses opened her up to the beauty of community, to how genuine relationship invites healing.

Before I got back from the cross-country meet, one of her friends had asked her to a movie, another to a football game for the next day, and still another to go bike riding and spend the night the day after.

And as we processed the letdown together, she was honest with herself and me. "You know," she said, "I could have practiced more before tryouts. Next time"—Yes, she said "next time"!—"I will know to work harder on the front end." I loved that she realizes a setback doesn't mean it's time to quit.

Then in a pinch-me moment as we sat at dinner that night, she thoughtfully digested the disappointment and took it a step further. "I can't believe I didn't make the team," she lamented honestly. "But I really am okay. I know it will be hard, but I will get through it."

She took a bite of her taco and continued, "It's weird because making a team sort of decides who you are. People put you with a group, and that's who you become. The volleyball player or the band member or TAG or whatever. And the truth is, I don't like how those things define you." She thought for a minute, then hit it home, "I kind of wish we would know people for who they are, not for what they do."

Thoughtful insight for a teen—or any of us. "I kind of wish we would know people for who they are, not for what they do."

I hope I'm taking notes.

Letting Go of Comparison

The urge to maintain appearances chains us to performance and leads us away from contentment. Freedom comes when we each focus on doing our best rather than being the best.

Great Expectations

Navigating Life's Detours

> My happiness grows in direct proportion to
> my acceptance, and in inverse proportion
> to my expectations.
>
> —Michael J. Fox

*L*ast night my niece stopped by for a chat. At age twenty-four she is perched, ready to take off and soar into life. Soaring is what we're supposed to do in our twenties, right?

"I'm just not so sure about everything," Shelley sighed as she sank into our couch. She's been working night shifts. Two nights on, one off, one on. First-year RNs get the tough schedules. So, while adjusting to irregular sleep habits, she's been learning all the ins and outs of the ICU. Needless to say, her mind and body are taxed to the max.

Her road to an RN degree wound through two years of community college, followed by two years at the nursing school. She knew her college experience was different than that of most of her friends who attended big-name universities upon graduating from high school. But taking a different path hadn't mattered to Shelley, who was determined to reach for her dreams by whatever means she could muster. It wasn't easy. With limited resources she entered the Dallas County Community College District and set her mind on the goal—Baylor nursing school.

Shelley achieved so much more than she imagined possible. Having graduated at the top of her class after putting herself through school on baby-sitting income and a full-ride scholarship, she landed one of the top jobs at Baylor University Medical Center.

But life has a way of not quite aligning with our expectations, even when we exceed our own goals. After all those long nights of study and work, Shelley had expected that, on crossing the finish line, she'd be rewarded with a terrific job, financial freedom, increased leisure time, and finally time to pursue a relationship.

Because that's how it works, right?

"What's not to be sure about?" I asked.

"You know, it's just not what I'd imagined." She rubbed her tired eyes and continued, "I imagined it all a little different. Like, the work thing is so rewarding in many ways, but so hard. Just not what I expected." Swallowing a yawn, she continued, "I thought I would jump in, and it would all run smooth like clockwork. When I was in school, I wanted to be out and on the floor."

As she talked, I remembered myself at her age, eager to dive in to the "real" world. Then sinking into a little disappointment as reality set in and I realized that work is every day, based on someone else's schedule. It wasn't quite what I had dreamed either. Especially since my first office was the copy room. (Imagine the fun of answering repeated "What's that sound in the background?" questions.) No worries, my time in the copy room didn't last too long. I George Jeffersoned right on up within months—to my firm's newly created Kay's office/ File Room. Yeah, me and the files. Livin' the dream.

Shelley continued. "I just hadn't calculated into the equation the fact that I will almost always have something new I need to be learning. So I'm still studying, even though I thought that would all be over. And the physicality. I expected to be working night shifts. But physically it's so much harder than I imagined. Especially when most of my friends work regular schedules. When they go grab dinner, I'm headed to work—or I'm exhausted."

Personally, I can't imagine how night shifters do it, though I'm eternally grateful for the highly skilled folks who do, especially at a hospital.

"But the physical doesn't hold a candle to the emotional challenges." She's been at it for six months, so is still on the steep slope of this learning curve in life. "I knew I would love getting to help people. But even that is so much more than I imagined. I just wish I had more time with the families. By the time they get to my floor, their family member is literally fighting for life. I didn't realize how deeply I could care for strangers, and it's . . . uhmmm . . . well, it's really special, but *so* hard."

I truly enjoy my conversations with this insightful young woman. I hope my kids will be as thoughtful and purposeful in their own walks into adulthood.

She continued talking about her patients and their families. "I didn't expect how heavy a burden that can be. These aren't happy stories. They're hard and so full of pain and sadness. I've had to find a way to leave work at work. I can't take it home with me. It's just too much. So I've started to ask the families if I can pray for them right there, in the moment. And that's helped so much. Somehow it relieves the burden I feel for them."

She continued to describe her life outside work, her roommates, her love life. And about how, though good, most of it was not quite what she'd anticipated. "Okay, so here's where I just don't know what to think," she returned to where she had started. "Not much is like I expected. And it's hard to not be overwhelmed by it all."

"I hear you," I commiserated and tried to share a little of what I've learned. "When Jon and I first got married, it was hard." I chuckled as I remembered back eighteen years ago to our little "dream" house that wasn't quite where I had imagined myself living. Only a chain-link fence separated the side of our house from the Dallas North Tollway, one of the busiest highways in Dallas. I called it our oceanfront property because, like waves hitting the sand, the hum of the traffic lulled us to sleep at night. During the day I got to see it all. Come five o'clock I could have had conversations with, or tossed a Coke over the fence to, the poor souls stuck in traffic.

The location of our house wasn't the problem. I was the issue. And my expectations didn't stop at living quarters.

"I had imagined marriage being a certain way," I confessed. "Both of us had fairly demanding jobs. So, exhausted by the time we got home, I struggled with self-imposed pressure to have dinner on the table. My mother always had dinner on the table for our family. So did Jon's. June Cleaver did for hers."

Shelley's slightly confused expression signaled her lack of name recognition. I think Carol Brady would have garnered the same reaction. But Carol had the answer. Staff. What I wouldn't have given for an Alice at my house, not only for the help but for friendship and reality checks.

"I had a small problem." I forged ahead with my story. "I did not know how to cook. Before getting married, I had never really been to the grocery store. I mean *really* gone to the grocery store, you know, to get more than milk, cereal, and peanut butter." I tried to ignore the pathetic nature of that admission. "I knew how to make waffles, though. And since someone had given us a waffle maker as a wedding gift, I cooked waffles at least three times a week for dinner—for almost six months. I hated those waffles after a while. Not just the way they tasted, but what they represented. Me and my inadequacies. And as the stress of my failure at being a wife built up, one night I lost it. I started bawling, which is hilarious. I'm not normally a crier. And I don't think guys really know what to do with a crying woman anyway, especially when it's about waffles."

Unexpected adventure makes for a better story.
—Lynn O'Rourke Hayes

"What did Uncle Jon do?" Shelley asked.

"It took him a minute to absorb the fact that no one had died. And that dinner really had made me that upset. Then he said, 'I don't care about dinner. You don't have to make me something. We can figure that out together.' I couldn't believe it. How could he not care about dinner? That was my *job*, right?"

Because that's how it works.

"I learned a lot about expectations that day. I thought he expected dinner on the table. He didn't. It was me. I had expectations in my mind of what life was supposed to look like. Dinner on the table for my husband was one. And I had let those expectations, the fact that they were unmet, literally suck the joy out of what should have been a really wonderful time. The reality that dinner could toy with my thoughts in such a powerful way floored me. And I swore to myself, I would never give expectations that kind of power again."

LEVELING LIFE'S U-CURVE

Expectations drive life. Stock prices soar or tank according to earnings expectations. Movie premier success is determined by box office receipts as compared to projected earnings (expectations). Job satisfaction is tied to exceeded or unmet expectations. Apparently my role as a wife carried an expectation that I didn't even know was there—until it went unmet.

It's interesting to me how assessments on which we base our expectations often don't match reality. My dinner expectations, though seemingly reasonable according to societal standards, had nothing to do with reality. Reality involved a husband who didn't care about my having dinner on the table when he got home from work. Who knew I could be so lucky? On the flip side, when I did make dinner—usually a crowd-pleasing casserole from one of my mother's recipes—it wasn't met with much enthusiasm. He didn't come from a casserole family and didn't bring with him an affinity for anything involving a can of cream of (fill in the blank) soup. (How can anyone live in Texas and not be a cream soup fan?!) At this point, good communication can save us from those unspoken, unfounded expectations—and the resulting discontent.

Despite how isolated we may feel amid the pressure of expectations, whether imposed by ourselves or others, we're not alone. Researchers have found that people tend to be happier in the early and later stages of life. Not so much in the middle. It seems as though expectations, specifically those of the unmet variety, are the major culprit.

Hannes Schwandt of Princeton's Center for Health and Wellbeing, along with other social scientists, embarked in 2013 on a major effort to study the theory of life's U-shape, which is seen across nationalities and socioeconomic groups. According to Schwandt, most people "expect—incorrectly—increases [in life satisfaction] in young adulthood and decreases during old age."[1] Here's what actually happens, according to the research: human beings are happy when they are in their very young adulthood and when they are hitting their sixties. But they experience quite low levels of well-being and life satisfaction during midlife, which thanks to "quarter-life crisis," is getting longer.

> Young adults have high aspirations that are subsequently
> unmet. And their life satisfaction decreases with age as long
> as expectations remain high and unmet. Aspirations are
> abandoned and expectations align with current wellbeing in
> the late 50s. This is the age when wellbeing starts to rise again.[2]

In other words, starting with the quarter-life crisis in their mid-twenties, people become increasingly frustrated as they compare reality to the ideal life they'd envisioned.

The apparent existence of life's U-shape isn't new and has sparked research from all over the world. And the U-shape isn't exclusive to the West. It doesn't pay much attention to financial well-being, lot in life, or where you live. *The Economist*, looking for the answer, reported:

> Americans and Zimbabweans have not been formed by similar experiences, yet the U-bend appears in both their countries. . . .
>
> Perhaps the U-bend is merely an expression of the effect of external circumstances. After all, common factors affect people at different stages of the life-cycle. People in their 40s, for instance, often have teenage children. Could the misery of the middle-aged be the consequence of sharing space with angry adolescents? And older people tend to be richer. Could their relative contentment be the result of their piles of cash?
>
> The answer, it turns out, is no: control for cash, employment status and children, and the U-bend is still there. So the growing happiness that follows middle-aged misery must be the result not of external circumstances but of internal changes. . . .
>
> Maybe people come to accept their strengths and weaknesses, give up hoping to become chief executive or have a picture shown in the Royal Academy, and learn to be satisfied as assistant branch manager, with their watercolour on display at the church fete.[3]

As I noted earlier, having goals and high aspirations is good. The issue is not aspiration. The issue is the way we react when expectations go unmet—and even when they are exceeded. Dreaming and aspiring keeps us striving for more, pursuing things that may be good for ourselves, our community, and the world. But ultimately our satisfaction rests in our ability to enjoy the spoils of success or deal with disappointment. Contentment comes, in large part, with acceptance and gratitude for what we do have, rather than focusing on all the unmet expectations and the accompanying pressures.

The so-called midlife crisis has almost everything to do with marinating our thoughts in the disparity between what we anticipated and what we've experienced, most often in the context of comparison to others. We get so focused on the way we think things should look, we forget to see all the good that is.

So if Jon comes home from a business trip and falls asleep on the couch—something slightly less than I might have anticipated, dare I say banked on, during my possibly long and arduous parenting week—sure, I can talk to him later about my week and how his failure to engage at home might be a downer for me and the kids. But first can I appreciate the fact that my husband comes home? That he has a job, though often stressful, that requires him to think and work diligently to find solutions for clients who actually need his specific talents? Can I be thankful that we have a more than adequate roof over our heads and a clean couch on which he can fall asleep? And that when his kids, even the teenagers, hear the door open to announce his return, they still run to hug their dad?

That's good stuff.

When I focus on all the unmet expectations surrounding his couch moment *(Seriously, the guy's asleep? Does he have any idea the week I've had and how badly I could use a break?),* irritation festers and resentment seethes, potentially leading to an ugly conflict. I just might experience a touch of envy as I envision my friend Ann's home and her husband who steps up at just the hint of a need. Granted, I don't know if that's what actually happens, but it sure seems like it. Are my thoughts justified? Maybe a couple. But I think I'd rather pursue the bonus inherent in Schwandt's conclusion: People might not "anticipate the wellbeing enhancing effects of abandoning high aspirations and experiencing less regret."[4] Which I think is some supersmart person's way to say, "Don't worry. Be happy."

White-knuckle gripping our unmet expectations tends to ignite frustration, fear, sometimes even anger. By contrast, acceptance of those unmet expectations, and actively noting the good things we enjoy in spite of life's shortcomings, fosters happiness.

> Researchers have found that people who regularly write down things for which they are grateful in "gratitude journals" have increased satisfaction in life, higher energy levels, and improved health. In one study, people who read a letter of appreciation to someone in their lives were measurably happier almost one month later. Performing acts of kindness or altruism boosts moods.[5]

In other words, letting go of our comparisons and choosing to be happy anyway can actually alleviate stress and improve our health.

Even the simple act of smiling stimulates peace and contentment. According to researchers, "neurotransmitters called endorphins are released when you smile."

These are triggered by the movements of the muscles in your face, which is interpreted by your brain, which in turn releases these chemicals. Endorphins are responsible for making us feel happy, and they also help lower stress levels. Faking a smile or laugh works as well as the real thing—the brain doesn't differentiate between real or fake as it interprets the positioning of the facial muscles in the same way.[6]

I'm reminded yet again of my grandmother and her gentle chides: "Smile. You'll feel better." And I try to remind my kids that being happy is a choice, though my reminding is often in a moment when all is wrong in their world, like the Legos not fitting together. But the principle still applies.

Expectation issues are real. Managing them takes practice. Remember the famous Serenity Prayer: "God, grant me the serenity to accept the things I cannot change, the courage to change the things I can, and the wisdom to know the difference."[7]

How Things Are Supposed to Be

I can get tripped up by unmet expectations. Clearly my birthday this year would fall in that category. But I'm pretty certain those sharing life with me could too. Though I spent much of my younger days running around a tennis court, riding bikes, hiking, or doing anything outdoor and active, my idea of recreation these days involves a chair next to a body of water. Hmm . . . I wonder how that might be getting under Jon's "let's go hit a few tennis balls" skin.

> **This is my "depressed stance." When you're depressed, it makes a lot of difference how you stand. The worst thing you can do is straighten up and hold your head high because then you'll start to feel better. If you're going to get any joy out of being depressed, you've got to stand like this.**
> —Charlie Brown

Marriage offers ample opportunities for expectations to toy with us. But so does almost every other aspect of life. I remember the same struggle in my banking career and in the political world fighting for the right spin. Parenting certainly brings a plethora of expectations. It's loaded with opportunities to compare what we've got to the way it should be, not only according to ourselves and our preconceived ideas, but according to all the books that tell us how it's supposed to work, and all the family members and friends who know how to do it right, and the kids themselves, who have plenty of opinions too.

When I was pregnant with our first child, I read the books. I looked at the pictures. I heard from friends who had already started families. Jon and I never struggled with infertility, so I can only imagine the difficulties in handling those unmet expectations. As the kids grew, we quickly learned that there is no one, right way to parent. Maybe that's where faith and trust enter the picture to help us weather the storms. I'm grateful that the Lord never asks for perfection, far from it.

"Sometimes I find myself considering my life as a picture I've created in my mind. Then I wait for the Lord to make it happen." My friend and I were walking this morning. She was telling me about a conversation she had with another mother about all the things we think we have to do to look or to be okay. Our conversation was spurred by contemplating out loud our busy lives and those things we think make the best environment for our families.

I told her about a blog sweet Jen Hatmaker had posted on parenting teens. In reading it I was moved, like thousands of others, by the beautiful picture she painted and the photos she shared. Her inspiring message that all the seeds you plant when your kids are little will produce wonderful kids—even in the teen years—was encouraging.

But as I looked at the smiling photos, I couldn't help but think, "Glad that has worked for you." Because even though we've been planting and watering and fertilizing, our home often doesn't look the way it's *supposed* to look. And I searched my mind to confirm that yes, we did and do plant positive seeds, we've done our best to "do it right," but a real-life photo album of an average day at the Wyma house wouldn't always feature smiley, happy people.

My walking friend's experience is similar.

"We were just talking about this the other morning," she told me. She still meets with the same group of moms she first connected with when her now-college-age kids were in grade school. Each one of the families represented had "done it right," as best they knew *and* according to expert advice. But the formulas didn't yield the expected outcomes. "We raised our boys, prayed over our boys, steered them to excellence and good decisions, and the truth is, some are striving and some are flailing."

I found comfort in her honesty. I think we can often feel alone, like we're the only ones struggling.

And it stings like judgment when I'm hit with confident declarations of what it means to do things "right," not only by blog posts or books but also from well-meaning folks with their admonitions to pursue things differently. The truth is, there are practical methods— many of which I saw take hold during our year of putting responsibility on our kids' plates—that fit in the "so that it may go well with you"[8] category. And I've witnessed, lived, and shared many of the good expected outcomes. But I've also shared the bad and ugly when methods aren't playing out quite like we hoped, even though we're trying our best. (At least, I think we're trying our best.) It's those times I want to yell, "Come live my life for a few days, and then you can judge me!" Because learning that some crops take longer to flourish can be a painful process in this instant-results-oriented world.

I think this idea of "the right way" is a canvas we, with help from well-intentioned wisdom givers, create in our minds. We paint a mental picture of how things are supposed to turn out and the landmarks that will prove our lives are on track to their intended destinations. I have one such picture in my mind for each of my children, as well as one for me—and one for Jon too, if I'm honest. My mental picture isn't a Pollyanna painting; I envision plenty of bumps along the way to give the landscape depth and dimension, some shadows to contrast with the light. But even so, I expect our lives to follow a particular pattern. That's how it works, right? You do certain things that produce certain results.

"Once my sister-in-law asked me," my friend continued, "'What would you want your life to look like if it could be anything?' And I really thought about her question."

"Interestingly enough," she said, "up to then, *that* was the problem. I had a way I wanted my life to be. And when reality didn't look that way, I was discontent and frustrated. Maybe even angry."

My friend continued, "What I've learned is, it's not bad to want my life to look a certain way. I can pray specifically for such things, but I need to hold them loosely. I want to give God a blank canvas. Let Him paint it. Then rest in the fact that the painting will never look like what I plan, and I'm grateful for it."

I think she's right. It isn't wrong to have goals and hopes and dreams. Or to work diligently toward such things. But when those expectations determine our contentment, we may have a problem. Because things usually don't end up the way we think they will.

One of my kids is studying Impressionist artists at the moment. "Dot, dot, Georges Seurat," Manet, Monet—artists who used an interesting technique of small brush strokes that viewed up close could appear nonsensical. But when we step back to see the variety of strokes as a whole, we are amazed at how the very small strokes work together to create a masterpiece.

"The painting isn't finished," my friend said, as we turned the corner and headed home. "I can't see it all. And why does it work for some and not for others? Why do their pictures appear instantly and mine seems like a flawed Polaroid? I don't know. But the truth, the one I usually don't want to hear, is that I don't have to know. But I do have to trust. I must trust that putting one foot in front of the other is enough. And to keep putting one foot in front of the other. My part is obedience."

> ### God always gives his best to those who leave the choice with him.
> —Jim Elliot

I love it. Blank canvas living.

Well, I love it and am scared of it at the same time. As it relates to me, I can live with it. But add my kids to the equation, and I sometimes forget to breathe.

TRAVELING THE UNMARKED ROADS

Detours from the expected are part of life. And the way we handle them has a huge effect on our outlook and our contentment. We can either be miserable, frustrated complainers, or we can make the detour a high-road excursion. Unwanted change doesn't have to land us in a ditch.

On a recent Tuesday, Fury stepped on a bee. He screamed and wailed so loud, one of the neighbor kids told me yesterday, "Yeah, I heard him from *my* front yard." (Embarrassing.) Fury is actually a pretty tough kid. But that bee nailed him right in the tender spot on the bottom of his foot, and the sting just kept coming.

I quickly removed the stinger and applied a baking-soda paste to ease the pain. We tried to distract him with a game of Mexican Trains. And all seemed well. In fact he was quick to join some friends at Lil Ninjas Gym, our new favorite staycation outing, soon after.

But later, in the middle of the night, when he stood next to my bed, begging for help with the pain, I realized this might not be a simple sting. And by the end of the next day, it was clear we needed to visit the doctor. Not only was he having an allergic reaction, he had an infection, staph at that. Thankfully, we have access to great medical care and antibiotics. The kid was soon on the mend.

Still, the incident sort of ruined his plans for the next week since he could barely walk, let alone run and play. He was on a bit of a detour. Of course, I hoped he would use the time to finish the summer reading assignment (doubtful). And though he was bummed, truly disappointed, he met the challenge head on, hopping around with very little complaining, despite the pain and plan changes.

On the flip side, yesterday afternoon I was with another one of my children who has also been dished a plate of change. Boxster is facing a school year that will look almost 100 percent different from what he hoped for and expected from his senior year. A couple of our kids attend a small school where they enjoy close relationships with their teachers. So when change, in the form of faculty departures, was announced last May, this child took it especially hard.

I'm moved that a kid could share such deep and meaningful relationships with teachers. On the reality side, however, what can you say but "Welcome to life." Accepting unexpected circumstances is part of the package. After acknowledging his sadness over unmet expectations,

I told him it's time to move on. Isn't that part of the mom job?! Life lecture? Probably not, but I do it anyway.

"Few things in life are certain," I told him as we sat outside Chipotle. "One of them is change. Some of it's good and brings with it a load of happiness. Some of it is challenging and not quite what we expect or hope. But you *are not* a victim. It happens to everybody, every day."

Then I added what I really hoped he could hear, "*You* get to choose your response. And the way you handle change will be a determining factor in your happiness."

I think it really is.

Detours occur. Change is inevitable. My perspective, my attitude, and my response are key. I can choose to wallow in frustration, anger, and disappointment. Or I can meet change head on, treat the symptoms, get help if needed, accept what I can't change—and hop around until my foot returns to normal. Or until I get used to my new normal.

Letting Go of Comparison

Expectations find life through comparison and drag us down the road to discontent. Learning to accept life as it comes frees us to recognize an unexpected path on our route to our happiness. Because "a truly happy person is one who can enjoy the scenery on a detour" (Author Unknown).

12

Dare We Not Compare?

Staking Our Claim in the Land of Contentment

I have learned the secret of being content . . .

—the apostle Paul

*I*n our house it was a challenge that came in the form of "I'll try" from Snopes as she contemplated the potential effects of being happy for others. Could it be the key to contentment? Can we be free from comparison pressures—the kind that accompany expectations, perceptions, our incessant obsession with what others are doing or have? Could peeling our eyes away from ourselves in order to see the world around us and all the people in it, actually be the answer?

It sure has helped.

Personally, I've found that shifting my focus has transformed how I navigate life. My kids have benefited too. But it is a constant challenge, one in which I often need reminders to mentally reboot.

As we've become aware of our tendency toward Greater Than/Less Than thinking, our eyes have opened to the richness of life smack dab in front of us—mostly in the form of the people with whom we're sharing it.

Being able to say "I'm happy for you" is not merely about celebrating someone else but about escaping the prison of dissatisfaction built by the bars of self-centered thinking. As we deliberately pursue compassion rather than comparison, we find our lives enlarged. Contentment isn't something yet to be found out there; it's right here with us, ready to be enjoyed.

Just the other day in the car, I overheard a sister telling a brother, "Quit thinking about how everyone else is going to do." It could have been in reference to a cross-country workout or a test; I don't know. But I must admit, I love hearing such pep talk—proof that they actually care about each other, especially when our usual less-edifying forms of conversation include yelling or whining or declarations of unfairness. As brief as the moment might be, I was soaking it in.

She continued, "Just do your best. You can't do anything more than that. Then look up for a minute. Someone standing next to you is feeling the same pressure you do. Try saying something funny. You're hilarious. You can get their mind off themselves too."

So yes, "I'm happy for you," in all its trading self-obsession for consideration of others, has fueled our bumbling efforts to throw off the entangling weight of comparison. Though we haven't fully succeeded, we're now much more aware of comparison's power to discourage, and we're also on alert for ways we can counteract it. And we're not the only ones. My friend Julie Hildebrand is taking on comparison as a dare. A dare to not compare.

Every year I make New Year's resolutions. The clean slate of the New Year is the perfect opportunity to do things better, work harder, and strive to better myself. But this year I'm having a hard time making a long list of resolutions I can put my whole heart into. And I think that's a good thing.

It's not that I've achieved perfection, to be sure. No, it's just that I'm looking at resolutions in a different light this year, hopefully a healthier light. As I listed the typical New Year's resolutions, most fell into the categories of body image and money with the underlying theme, "Whatever is now is not good enough."

Admittedly, "not good enough" is a plausible conclusion as we are bombarded hundreds of times a day with messages encouraging us to be discouraged about our current situation. Billboards, TV ads, social media, and Pinterest show us what we are missing out on in life—and just how great things could be if we only had what they are peddling. Without making a conscious decision to do so, we compare our lives with the unrealistic, staged messages the world is constantly throwing at us. And we come up short every time. Or maybe it's just me.

And so, this year, my New Year's resolution will be different. I am going to resolve to do something I've been encouraging my kids to do lately. As my children have been plagued by comparison with each other, with friends or strangers, I've repeated to them, "Stop comparing your life with someone else's. We all have our own race. Stay in your own lane."

I've said it out of love, explaining to my kids that God created each of them for a unique purpose. And as their mother, I know that if they spend their time in constant comparison, they will not be the people God created them to be and will not live the abundant life God intended for them.

And so it is with me. I do not want comparison to steal my joy or derail me from the path the Lord has set for me. Therefore, I resolve in the year ahead to stay in my own lane. Run my own race. Stop comparing.

While it is so easy to slip into comparison mode, it can be difficult to stand firm in the truth. And the truth is, God loves us with an unending love, and He does not compare us one with another. As a matter of fact, I read something recently that became a comparison game changer. Author Henri Nouwen wrote in his book *The Return of the Prodigal Son,* "Our God . . . does not compare. Never. . . . I cannot fathom how all of God's children can be favorites. And still, they are. . . . God loves with a divine love, a love that cedes to all women and men their uniqueness without ever comparing."

I read the quote above and my heart rejoices and the weight comes off of my shoulders. How different from what the world says is true. How different from "not good enough." I am God's favorite. And so are you. And so are our children.

And so are all of His children. He does not compare, and neither should we. Living as God's favorite makes living in comparison futile, if not downright silly.

I don't want to be futile or silly this year. So, while there is value in taking inventory of our lives each new year and making necessary changes and improvements, we must be careful not to fall into the pit of "never good enough" as a result of constant comparison. No more striving, no more hustling, we are enough as we are right now. Sin-stained, imperfect, unPhotoshopped, we are enough to be loved by God and by others.

We are each His favorite. And that's the truth.

A new year doesn't have to begin on January 1. It can begin any day. Time moves too quickly to wait.

If a Kid Can Do It, So Can I

We get chances to practice every day. Today, high school volleyball practice started. School starts next week. Anxiety levels are high.

Lots of families eagerly embrace the beginning of school. Our family greets it like a prison sentence. Granted, the kids love getting to see their friends. They actually adore their teachers. I think they enjoy the structure—a little.

But generally speaking, blank calendar days rock our world. All of us, but perhaps I most of all, revel in the freedom from calendar stress. But it does come to an end and school sports begin.

"So how was it?" I asked Snopes when she got into the car.

"Well, it was so incredibly hot. The air conditioner wasn't working in the gym. I've never been so hot."

"Oh, I bet they'll get that fixed. Nobody has been using the gym over the summer, so they probably didn't even know."

"I hope they get it fixed," she said, literally drenched from head to toe. "But it's all right."

We drove out of the parking lot. I resisted the urge to stop and chat with a couple of moms I hadn't seen in a while. I'm working on talking less.

"Was practice fun?"

"Yeah. I was super nervous that I had forgotten everything. But I haven't." She paused. "Coach made me the setter."

I know nothing about volleyball except that I like to watch the games. It's such a happy sport. Everyone works together. No one is taking something from someone. And they cheer for each other all the time. Even when they lose a point, they cheer each other on. It's the Disney World of sporting events.

"Well, that's terrific," I respond.

"It isn't," she replied. "In fact, to be honest with you, I was kind of frustrated. At least at first. Until I thought about it."

Huh?

"There's something about getting to be at the net spiking. It's . . . well . . ."

"The accolades?"

"No, it's . . . uh . . ."

"Getting to hit the ball hard and win the point?"

"No, it's . . . well . . . it's when people cheer."

"That's accolades." I smiled.

"Whatever." She eye-rolled. "Anyway, no one ever notices the setter. The setter is the only player on the court who touches the ball every single point, but never wins a point. The truth is, no one cheers for the setter. And"—she stammered through the next words—"I like it when people cheer for me."

Her honesty never fails to astound me.

"It feels good when people cheer for you," she continued. "Then I thought about all the girls on the court with me and how great they must feel when people cheer for them. Then"—her excitement started to flow—"I started to realize what a great spot the setter job is. Oh my word! My whole role will be setting people up to feel good. I couldn't believe it. It's perfect. It feels so much better to set people up to be cheered than to be the one cheered."

She's absolutely right.

"It feels so much better to set people up to be cheered than to be the one cheered."

Seriously. Who is the adult in this scenario?!

The heaviness of setting ourselves up to be cheered, to be rewarded, to be noticed, to be something is staggering. It's a full-time, never-ending job.

Contrast that to the lightness of setting others up to be cheered. It's counterintuitive to think that greater reward comes from cheering others than from gaining accolades. And yet consider how it frees us from the layers that weigh us down.

That's what being happy for someone does. It shifts our energy and attention from what we don't have to what we can appreciate and celebrate.

PRACTICE MAKES PERFECT. MAYBE NOT PERFECT, BUT IT REMINDS ME TO BREATHE.

My grandmother used to tell me, "In order to have a friend, you need to be a friend." Which I found true to a certain extent. But as Snopes learned in her role as setter, my attention quickly turned from the motivation of simply having friends to the unexpected satisfaction that came from being a friend.

Dr. David Henderson, director of counseling at Criswell College, described the seven people waiting when you fall, one of which is a friend. A friend, according to Dr. Henderson, is "the person who is loyal and genuinely wants you to succeed in life. You know them by how willing they are to celebrate with you when you're succeeding, not just by how they help you up when you've fallen."

He goes on to ponder the benefits derived not only from having but from being such a friend. These benefits range from the wisdom you naturally glean from walking through life together, to increased credibility, to gaining a future ally. But what really caught my eye was *the sense of purpose you feel*. "When you learn to celebrate with others, you discover the true purpose for living life."[1]

Celebrate and commiserate. Both of which begin with seeing beyond ourselves and how life relates to us and looking with care and concern at those with whom we share life.

Since this attempt to tame comparison began with my eyes being opened to its destructive and peace-stealing nature in the parenting realm, why not end there? Though I think we've seen that comparison strikes everywhere, its effects concern me most in the area of parenting because that happens to be where I live—at least for the next few years. I know I will be a parent for the rest of my life, but as the kids get older, I care less and less about societal noise.

For me, today, at this very moment, comparison finds traction in college applications. And I fight being sad and glad for things like social media. In days gone by, rarely were any of us privy to so much personal information. Now we get a Glimpse into almost every detail. And even though I genuinely know better, I can't believe the pit that hits my stomach the moment I see pics of school acceptances and National Merit Scholarships and new cars and so much more posted by families whose paths cross ours.

A part of me is glad I have to fight to breathe and to be excited for these families. At least I know I'm normal. Because that's what the struggle with comparison is—normal. Not normal as we try to define people, but as in regular life. Comparing has been around since the beginning, and it's most certainly here to stay, in some form or fashion.

So what do I do?

Breathe.

And remember—I have to remember—everyone else's seemingly gold-paved road is a Glimpse. Then I force my thoughts to center on our child, whose unique giftedness will most certainly put him on a path that's different from the ones a lot of his friends are on. While they are leaning into all the excitement of fraternities, football games, and college parties, posting pics and witty quips, my kid will most likely be with a small group of problem solvers. Spending their free time figuring out how Aristotle's ideas can be quantified. Honestly, I have no idea what types of equations will capture his thoughts, but I know—especially after savoring his geometric-equation dinner drawings—something will. And I also know that this world will be a better place because of him, a thoughtful philosopher who has figured out that mathematics makes the world go around. So I strain to see the big picture and put my eggs in the long-term basket. Rather than have my joy sapped by what looks so perfect and easy in *everyone* else's life.

Breathing reminds me to be grateful. Thankful for a kid who has character, who takes the high road, who refuses to compromise, whose work ethic is nothing short of admirable. Then I reach for some perspective to help me focus on reality, not on expectations. And with perspective, I tap into faith. Faith that everything actually does work together for good.

And with that, contentment enters the picture.

Only then can we peel our thoughts away from self-absorption and be able to see those with whom we share life. And not simply see them but fully embrace the life we live *with* instead of *against* each other.

Then, with some extra oxygen pulsing through my veins thanks to some life-giving breaths, I revisit a few of the insightful perspectives mentioned earlier by those who have walked the road ahead of us, because I don't want to forget:

> We should love men enough not to envy, and this is not only
> envy for money; it is for everything. —Francis Schaeffer

Lower your expectations of earth. This isn't heaven; so don't expect it to be. —Max Lucado

To be nobody-but-yourself—in a world which is doing its best, night and day, to make you everybody else—means to fight the hardest battle which any human being can fight; and never stop fighting. —e. e. cummings

When you learn to celebrate with others, you discover the true purpose for living life. —David Henderson

Suppose we can see the successes, the accomplishments, the victories of others as [God's] gifts also. That puts them in a different light. . . . When I'm doing that, I discovered, it's hard to keep on envying them. I find myself beginning to celebrate, to rejoice in, what God is doing through them. And that's a victory I could never win by myself. It's a gift of grace. —William Brownson

How nice that Dr. Brownson points to ultimate relief. He provides insight into the hardest part of being happy for someone: *meaning it*. The truth is, I want to be happy for you, but I'm not sure I consistently can. I'm not sure I can do it even for a few minutes.

Grateful for his recognition that "It's a gift of grace," I can sink into the fact that left to myself I can't do it. And I'm thankful to know I don't have to.

We've had a full harvest moon this week in Dallas. Stunning in its display, the magnificent sphere begs every eye to see it. Suffice it to say, I might have missed a few turns and narrowly escaped a couple of fender benders as I've been distracted by its staggering beauty.

"Hey, look through the trees. Do you see it?" I asked Barton on our way home from dropping her brother at a friend's house.

"See what?"

"Oh my word! The moon! It's crazy beautiful!"

Slightly annoyed by my excited pestering, she looked up from her iPod. "Wow. It really is amazing."

"I know."

"It looks like it's so close that I could touch it."

"It does, doesn't it?"

"Wow. And it's brighter than the streetlights."

It was.

"I've never seen anything like it," she oohed, leaning into her inherited superlative reflex, completely mesmerized, no longer aware of the Instagram pics that had held her attention, surrendering to the beauty blazing before her.

At this point, I couldn't stop myself from steering both of us toward truth. "You know the moon, on its own, has no light. Really no life. For all effective purposes, it's just a gigantic inanimate rock, tethered to the earth by gravitational pull.

"Any light that we see coming from the moon," I continued, "is only a reflection of the sun's light. Since tonight is a full moon, every part of it is reflecting the sun. It's as if the moon is fully surrendered to the sun. And it's almost as bright as the sun. When I woke up this morning, I thought I had left a light on in our bathroom all night. But it wasn't a light bulb; it was the moon shining through the window."

She was listening, so I kept going. "You know, that's like us when we fully surrender to God—we shine. And the shine is never our own. The more we surrender, the more we bask in His light and the more we reflect His light."

I stopped there. We both needed to chew on it a bit. I thought about the secret of life: serving and loving others. "I'm happy for you."

I thought about its power. I considered the fact that every time we opt for other-centeredness, every time we serve—genuinely serve, with no ulterior motives—it's like drinking a power shot. It's Snopes, the setter, walking off a volleyball court, filled rather than depleted. It's the person next to Snopes, spilling over onto someone else, spreading the *filled.*

"I'm happy for you."

Unconventional power that looks nothing like the bill of goods our culture sells. Culture tells us to do everything we can to get ahead. Culture tells us to self-promote. Culture tells us to manage our own interests, even suggests that volunteering might serve those interests. It tells us to take no prisoners, to win at all costs.

Our culture forgets to tell us that doing all those things actually lands us in a type of prison. Just like the one I struggled to avoid when bumping up against *everyone else's* college acceptances. Just like the one that handcuffed Adam and Eve when they bought into the idea that the provision all around them wasn't enough.

That the moon's mesmerizing light diverted my passenger's

attention from Instagram, so often a teen's gauge of likability and acceptance, and directed it instead toward such beauty offered us both a reminder as we sat for several minutes lost in its magnitude.

The reflective moon reminds me that I don't ever have to fight for contentment on my own, alone. The source of power—to mentally reboot, refocus perspective, be grateful, manage expectations, and be genuinely happy for others—comes from God, who does it for us. As the sun's light effectively powers the moon to shine, so also does God's light (the grace to which Brownson refers) power us to be able to genuinely celebrate and serve others, the secret to a truly rich life. And like the moon in all its glory, unaffected by society and its obsession with stealing our joy, I can surrender and rest in the true contentment that comes with loving others.

And that leads me to one more insightful perspective from someone who has walked the road ahead:

I know what it is to be in need, and I know what it is to have plenty. I have learned the secret of being content in any and every situation, whether well fed or hungry, whether living in plenty or in want. I can do all this through him who gives me strength.[2]

Discussion Questions

Chapters 1–2

1. How do you define comparison? Do you agree with Theodore Roosevelt's definition? Why does comparison rob us of joy? How have you seen this to be true in your own life?

2. In what ways does our society encourage us to compare ourselves to others?

3. On which areas of your life (work, family, friends, kids, etc.) do comparison temptations prey? How might a mental reboot (Ctrl-Alt-Delete from chapter 2) help you regain perspective? What are some practical ways you can shift from comparison to compassion in the heat of the moment?

Chapters 3–5

4. Have you ever experienced Glimpse comparison moments? When and where? What are some specific actions you can take to see beyond the moment?

5. Through which lenses do you tend to view life: in the moment or beyond the now, as it relates to yourself or as it relates to others, short-sighted or long-sighted? Which lenses offer insights that lead to contentment, and how might gratitude play a role?

6. How does concern about what others think of us drive our choices and behaviors? How might the fact that everyone else

struggles with what others think of them offer freedom from comparison pressure and opportunity to encourage others?

7. How does your view of how you look affect your daily life? Do you struggle with outward appearance pressure or body image issues? If yes, how? If no, what kind of practical steps do you take to keep these at bay?

Chapters 6–8

8. How would you define yardstick living? Describe a season or area in your life where you have felt pressure to measure up. What are some ways to navigate measuring lines while maintaining contentment?

9. In chapter 7, Kay quotes Steven Marche, who describes today's "world consumed by ever more novel modes of socializing" as "unprecedented alienation." To what extent can you relate to this description? How would you say social media and Internet connectedness affect interpersonal relationships? What practical things can we do to offset any negative impacts?

10. Does the concept of "fair" play a role in your life? What two attributes of fair does Kay describe in chapter 8? How might these play out in your own life? How does trust enter the picture?

Chapters 9–11

11. How are the side-to-side glances described by Kay different than the Glimpse in chapter 3? Kay quotes her friend Robin Pou as saying, "When we are focused on wanting what someone else

has, we've . . . substituted our unique giftedness for theirs" (page 163). What does this look like in your life?

12. Do you ever find yourself being glad about someone else's misfortune? What do those feelings reveal about what you value the most? What are some ways you could combat those feelings when they come?

13. Where do you feel *branding* pressure in your life? In what areas, if any, do you feel driven to be the best rather than simply aiming for your personal best? What are some practical ways to find contentment in those situations? If that's not an issue for you, how can you encourage someone who is struggling with *best*?

14. In your life, how do expectations correlate to contentment? Where would you place yourself on life's U-shape? Where would you like to be? How can you get there and stay there?

Chapter 12 and Overall Thoughts

15. What does it feel like to belong somewhere? In what relationships or places do you feel known?

16. What does it look like to value people over presentation?

17. What surprised you about yourself as you read and discussed this book? What surprised you about God?

18. What do you think is "the secret" to being content?

Acknowledgments

This project was born from an idea. "What's the elephant in the room?" Ken Petersen asked as he, Laura Barker, Erik Wolgemuth, and I brainstormed about relevant topics.

"Well, that's easy," I said without hesitation. "Comparison." On social media, in school hallways, at the gym, in the grocery store checkout—everyone is sizing each other or ourselves up and wondering, *Is it enough? Am I enough?* "Comparison is definitely sucking the life out of people. I'm not sure anyone is immune."

And thus *I'm Happy for You* began. Granted, it took a little longer to cook than any of us expected—mostly due to the never-ending nature of this subject—but inspired by ahhhh-maaazing cover art (thank you, Mark Ford), we stayed the course.

So thank you, Ken, for keeping us focused.

Thank you, Laura, for keeping me on course and making me laugh.

Thank you, Erik, for, well, for everything.

Thanks to the WaterBrook Multnomah team and to Lovell-Fairchild for the incredible things you do.

Thanks to the folks who let me share their stories, even when our positions on certain life issues differ.

A special word of thanks to my husband, Jon, still the most trustworthy person I know, and to my amazing children. Words can't begin to describe the amount of love and admiration I feel for these people. I am honored to know them, let alone to live life with them.

Thank you, Tuesday gals, for contemplating comparison and contentment while keeping it real. Here's a shout-out to each and every one of you.

Thank you, sister friends (Chris Wills, Ann Silva, Nancy Brown, Alex Wagner, Lynne Schott, Erin Schryer, and Jane Jarrell) who have been my sounding boards and steady anchors when waves threaten to rock our boat.

Thanks to the knee-brigade led by Elizabeth Tamlyn. And to Jennifer Clouse, Nell Bush, Mary Clayton Wood, and Mandy Bagdanov for coming alongside.

Thanks to my siblings (David, Kathy, and Charles) and their spouses (Chris, Don, and Paula) for caring more than I do. And even more gratitude for my parents, Don and Sue Wills, who trained their kids by practicing what they preached: hospitality and a load of others-centered living.

Thanks to *all* the very kind folks who endure my typos and flakiness via the *Moat Blog*. I'd be *so* incredibly lonely walking this road without you.

Lastly, if there is any truth or wisdom in this book, it isn't mine. (I'm just along for the ride.) It's supplied by the Lord, who has so much more to share and gives generously without finding fault. Check out His story. We read the 1984 New International Version around our house.

—K

Notes

Chapter 1: Obsessive Comparison Disorder

1. Paul Angone, "7 Cures for Your Quarter-Life Crisis," *Relevant,* August 2013, www.relevantmagazine.com/life/7-cures-your -quarter-life-crisis.

Chapter 2: The Icebreaker

1. "Promoting, Individual, Family, and Community Connected-ness to Prevent Suicidal Behavior," Centers for Disease Control, www.cdc.gov/violenceprevention/pdf/suicide_strategic_direction _full_version-a.pdf.

2. Norm Cohen, "Feeling Worthless and Depression," PsychCentral, http://psychcentral.com/lib/worthlessness-and-depression /000339.

3. George N. Christodoulou, "Depression as a Consequence of the Economic Crisis," World Federation for Mental Health, October 10, 2012, 14, http://wfmh.com/wp-content/uploads/2013/11 /2012_wmhday_english.pdf.

4. Andy Stanley, "The Comparison Trap, Part 1—The Land of Er," Northpoint Community Church sermons, February 12, 2012, http://northpoint.org/messages/comparison-trap/the -land-of-er.

5. Theodore Roosevelt; Iyanla Vanzant, "Why Women Compete with One Another," Oprah's Lifeclass, www.oprah.com/oprahs -lifeclass/Why-Women-Compete-with-One-Another-Video; and Dorothy Corkille Briggs, *Your Child's Self-Esteem: The Key to Life* (New York: Doubleday, 1975), 213.

Chapter 4: Do You See What I See?

1. Jordan Shirkman, "How to Stop Comparing Everyone's High-light Reels with Your Life," *Jordan Shirkman,* May 21, 2013, http://jshirk.com/blog/highlight-reels.
2. Shaun Dreisbach, "How Do You Feel About Your Body?" *Glamour,* October 2014, www.glamour.com/health-fitness /2014/10/body-image-how-do-you-feel-about-your-body.
3. Courtney Reissig, "The Quest for a Bigger, Better, Cuter Pregnancy," *Christianity Today,* March 2013, www.christianity today.com/women/2013/march/quest-for-bigger-better-cuter -pregnancy.html.
4. Steve Bradt, "Wandering Mind, Not a Happy Mind," *Harvard Gazette,* November 2010, http://news.harvard.edu/gazette/story /2010/11/wandering-mind-not-a-happy-mind.
5. Matthew A. Killingsworth and Daniel T. Gilbert, "A Wandering Mind Is an Unhappy Mind," *Science* 330, November 12, 2010, www.sciencemag.org/content/330/6006/932.full.pdf?sid=a524 6292-23a4-40c4-91eb-37db3d811c07.
6. Brené Brown, "Want to be happy? Stop trying to be perfect," CNN Living, www.cnn.com/2010/LIVING/11/01/give.up .perfection.

Chapter 5: Mirror, Mirror

1. Christina Goyanes, "A Revealing Look at the Thigh Gap Surgery Trend," *Shape,* May 16, 2014, www.shape.com/lifestyle /mind-and-body/revealing-look-thigh-gap-surgery-trend.

2. "The Dove Campaign for Real Beauty," Dove, www.dove.us /Social-Mission/campaign-for-real-beauty.aspx; "Dove Real Beauty Sketches," YouTube, www.youtube.com/watch?v=Xpa OjMXyJGk.

3. Gallagher Flinn, "How Mirrors Work," How Stuff Works, August 5, 2009, http://science.howstuffworks.com/innovation /everyday-innovations/mirror.htm.

4. Shaun Dreisbach, "How Do You Feel About Your Body?" *Glamour,* October 2014, www.glamour.com/health-fitness /2014/10/body-image-how-do-you-feel-about-your-body.

5. Dreisbach, "How Do You Feel About Your Body?"

6. Dreisbach, "How Do You Feel About Your Body?"

Chapter 6: The Dangers of Yardstick Living

1. Philip Zimbardo, "The Power of Norms and Groups on Individuals: Parallels Between the Stanford Prison Experiment and Milgram's Obedience Research," *The Lucifer Effect,* www .lucifereffect.com/links_add_norms.htm.

2. Shawn Achor, *The Happiness Advantage* (New York: Crown, 2010), 40.

Chapter 7: We Belong . . . Together

1. Simon Sinak, *Start with Why* (New York: Penguin, 2009), 53

2. Stephen Marche, "Is Facebook Making Us Lonely?" *The Atlantic,* April 2012, www.theatlantic.com/magazine/archive/2012/05/is-facebook-making-us-lonely/308930.

3. Jan Anderson and Lee Raine, "The Internet of Things Will Thrive by 2025," Pew Research, May 2014, www.pewinternet.org/2014/05/14/internet-of-things.

4. Jamil Zaki, "What? Me Care? Young Are Less Empathic," *Scientific American,* December 2010, www.scientificamerican.com/article/what-me-care.

5. Andy Braner, "Table Talk: When Most People Think of Teenagers," *Moat Blog,* October 2012, www.themoatblog.com/2012/10/table-talk-when-most-people-think-of-teenagers-by-andy-braner.

Chapter 8: Fair Play

1. Dave Ramsey, "20 Things the Rich Do Every Day," DaveRamsey.com, www.daveramsey.com/blog/20-things-the-rich-do-every-day.

2. 1 Samuel 23:16–17.

Chapter 9: The Side to Side

1. Kay Wyma, "At a Swim Meet, a Ribbon for Everyone," *New York Times,* November 10, 2013, http://parenting.blogs.nytimes.com/2013/11/10/at-a-swim-meet-a-ribbon-for-everyone/?_r=0.

2. A. J. Jacobs, *The Year of Living Biblically: One Man's Humble Quest to Follow the Bible as Literally as Possible* (New York: Simon & Schuster, 2008), 27–28.

3. William C. Brownson, "Jesus Saves Us from the Green Monster," Words of Hope, February 1994, https://woh.org/word/radio/1994/02/20.

4. Francis Schaeffer, *True Spirituality* (Carol Stream, IL: Tyndale, 2001), 11.

5. Brownson, "Jesus Saves Us from the Green Monster."

Chapter 10: Best Practices

1. "Educated and Jobless: What's Next for Millennials?" *All Things Considered,* NPR, November 12, 2011, www.npr.org/2011/11/12/142274437/educated-and-jobless-whats-next-for-millenials.

2. Tom Peters, "The Brand Called You," *Fast Company,* August–September 1997, www.fastcompany.com/28905/brand-called-you.

3. Tom Peters, Twitter, https://twitter.com/tom_peters/status/418400315906326528.

4. Dorie Clark, "Brand You 2014: Five Personal Branding Tips for the Year Ahead," *The Guardian,* January 6, 2014, www.theguardian.com/media-network/media-network-blog/2014/jan/06/brand-you-2014-personal-branding-tips.

5. C. S. Lewis, *Mere Christianity* (New York: HarperCollins, 1980), 122.

6. See www.lifehack.org/articles/productivity/the-top-10-traps-that-stop-you-from-being-successful.html.

7. Seth Godin, interview by Bryan Elliott, "Behind the Brand," uploaded May 9, 2011, www.youtube.com/watch?v=Lhk9fGYGddg.

8. Genesis 11:1, 4.

9. Judy Batalion, "If Ivy League Is the End Game, I'm Not Sure I Want to Play," Motherlode, *New York Times,* April 1 2014, http://parenting.blogs.nytimes.com/2014/04/01/if-ivy -league-is-the-endgame-im-not-sure-i-want-to-play/?_php =true&_type=blogs&_r=0.

10. Sharmistha Das, "Hello Selfie, Bye Autograph," *The Telegraph*, August 17, 2014, www.telegraphindia.com/1140817/jsp/7days /18728263.jsp.

Chapter 11: Great Expectations

1. Hannes Schwandt, "Unmet Aspirations as an Explanation for the Age U-Shape in Human Wellbeing" (Discussion Paper No. 1229, The Centre for Economic Performance Publications Unit, United Kingdom, July 2013), 1, http://cep.lse.ac.uk/pubs /download/dp1229.pdf.

2. Schwandt, "Unmet Aspirations," 6.

3. "The U-Bend of Life," *The Economist,* December 2010, print edition, www.economist.com/node/17722567.

4. Schwandt, "Unmet Aspirations," 6–7.

5. "How Happiness Affects Your Health," ABC News, March 27, 2013, http://abcnews.go.com/blogs/health/2013/03/27/how -happiness-affects-your-health.

6. Jennifer Smith, "7 Benefits of Smiling and Laughing That You Didn't Know About," Lifehack, www.lifehack.org/articles /communication/7-benefits-smiling-and-laughing.html.

7. The authorship of the Serenity Prayer has been disputed, but research tells us that theologian Reinhold Niebuhr (1892–1971) wrote the prayer as early as 1937.

8. Deuteronomy 6:3.

Chapter 12: Dare We Not Compare?

1. David Henderson, "Five Benefits of Celebrating Others' Successes," *Finding Purpose Beyond Our Pain,* March 13, 2014, http://purposebeyondpain.com/2014/03/13/five-benefits-of-celebrating-others-successes.

2. The apostle Paul, writing in Philippians 4:12–13.

Raising Responsible Kids, One Eye-Roll at a Time

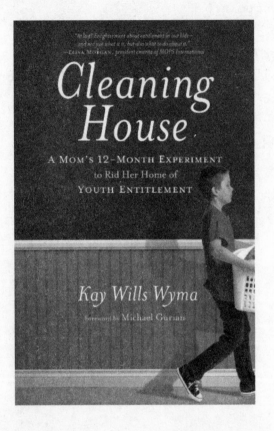

Dismayed at the attitude of entitlement that had crept into her home, Kay Wills Wyma got some attitude of her own. *Cleaning House* is her account of a year-long campaign to introduce her five kids to basic life skills and the ways meaningful work can increase earned self-confidence and concern for others.

Read an excerpt from this book and more at WaterBrookMultnomah.com!